THE FILMS OF ROBERT BRESSON

series edited and designed by Ian Cameron

THE FILMS OF
ROBERT BRESSON

AMEDEE AYFRE
CHARLES BARR
ANDRE BAZIN
RAYMOND DURGNAT
PHIL HARDY
DANIEL MILLAR
LEO MURRAY

PRAEGER

BOOKS THAT MATTER

*Published in the United States of America in 1970
by Frederick A. Praeger, Inc., Publishers, 111
Fourth Avenue, New York, N.Y. 10003*

© *1969 by Movie Magazine Limited*

*Library of Congress Catalog Card Number:
79–113413*

Produced by November Books Limited

Printed in England

*Amédée Ayfre's article is translated from the
chapter* 'L'Univers de Robert Bresson' *in*
'Conversion aux images?' (1964) *by permission
of the publishers, Les Editions du Cerf. André
Bazin's article originally appeared in* Cahiers du
Cinéma 3 *as* 'Le Journal d'un curé de campagne
et la stylistique de Robert Bresson', *and Hugh
Gray's translation is reprinted from the collection
of Bazin's essays,* 'What Is Cinema?' *by permission of the publishers, the University of California
Press. Raymond Durgnat's article on* Diary of a
Country Priest *is adapted from an article
published in* Films and Filming.

*The Editor wishes to thank Connoisseur Films for
the loan of 16mm copies of* Diary of a Country
Priest *and* Mouchette, *and the Academy Cinema
for screening* Une femme douce.

*Stills by courtesy of Academy Cinema,
Connoisseur, Contemporary, Mondial, National
Film Archive, Parc Films, Sebricon, Unifrance.*

This book consists of a series of essays by five
critics covering all Bresson's films from *Les
Anges du péché* to *Une femme douce.* In addition
there are two key texts on his work by two
French critics of an older generation, both now
dead. Amédée Ayfre's essay is used as an
introduction; although it covers only six of the
films, it remains the best general appreciation
of Bresson's work so far written. Finally there
is a brief interview on *The Trial of Joan of Arc*
which is intended to serve as a character sketch
of the director.

The two French articles are quoted elsewhere in the book, and there the translations
are those of the various authors – they may be
slightly at variance with the translations of the
whole article. Similarly biblical quotations have
been left in the forms preferred by the writers,
so that, for instance *'le vent souffle où il veut'*
appears in some places as 'the wind bloweth
where it listeth' and in others as 'the spirit
breathes where it will'.   I.A.C.

*Frontispiece: Bresson and Philippe Agostini
shooting the sequence at the Cascade in* Les
Dames du Bois de Boulogne.

CONTENTS

THE UNIVERSE OF ROBERT BRESSON

AMEDEE AYFRE

Bresson's total output is extremely limited compared to that of other film-makers of his generation: in twenty years [this article was written in 1962] he has made only six films. But, despite his wide range of subject matter, there are perhaps no films more unified or deeply marked by their director's personality. Undoubtedly the idea of the importance of the *auteur* in the cinema has been exaggerated by deliberately ignoring the often essential contribution of scriptwriters and adapters, of the producer, the editor, the cameraman, and sometimes the actors. The attempt to react against an anonymous commercial cinema, against the privileged position of stars, or against literary prejudice, has resulted in the director being given not simply an important role, but an exclusive one. However, what is clearly an exaggeration in most cases – particularly as regards the American cinema – is the pure and simple truth for Bresson. From *Les Anges du péché* to *The Trial of Joan of Arc*, whatever the point of departure of the film and the personalities of the people involved, whatever the theme or the characters, we always deal with the same universe, even though a relative evolution can be traced from film to film.

This is why it is not at all artificial to attempt an analysis of this universe as a whole and to try to isolate the parts which create its unity, instead of dealing with each film separately. In order to do this, we shall not concern ourselves with Robert Bresson as a person, nor with his psychology, but with what I shall call

his mythology as it is expressed through the medium of the cinema. This is in any case the best way of respecting the rich personality of a man who has always chosen to stay discreetly in the background and who hates nothing more than to make a public exhibition of himself. Besides, in so far as his universe constitutes a whole, it would be impossible to make separate studies of content and form. The subject matter as such is not particularly original: the cinema teems with stories of abandoned mistresses, reformed thieves, escaped prisoners, priests or nuns dedicated to saving souls, and warlike heroines who fall into enemy hands. Nor does analysis of isolated elements of Bresson's cinematographic language, stripped of their contextual significance, reveal more than curious quirks. Only by respecting the unfailing unity of themes and style can we really hope to get inside this universe and discover its richness and originality. So we must approach it through categories which do not rely exclusively on signs nor on meaning, but on both. Such categories, we feel, are the concepts of abstraction and reality, of stage character and real person, of loneliness and communication, and of immanence and transcendence.

From abstraction to reality

Bresson's universe is not that of everyday reality. It is distinct from it not only because it is an artistic universe, but because as such it makes no attempt to pass for the everyday universe. In this Bresson takes a different aesthetic position from others, who claim that they are setting up true works of art, yet define the truth of these works by direct reference to everyday life. When Zavattini and De Sica show us Umberto D going to bed or, in the same film, the maid getting up, they do it in order that we should witness gestures, attitudes and words which are often boring and insignificant as details, but which are interesting when seen as a whole, as they reveal a concrete situation to us, one which had never before attracted our attention. There is nothing like this in films such as *Les Dames du Bois de Boulogne* or *Pickpocket*. Nor indeed is there anything in these – or in any of Bresson's other films – which could be closely or remotely compared to the 'slice of life', to the documentary description of an environment or the concrete representation of a human reality. We are as far from *vérisme* and naturalism as from neo-realism. Are we then equally far from reality – in abstraction, for instance?

At this point it would be a good thing to define as closely as possible what is meant by reality and abstraction. Philosophers give the latter two quite distinct meanings. First, there is the abstraction which proceeds by extension and enables one to classify beings according to their most general characteristics: Man, Animal, Living, Being; or Commerce, Industry, Justice (the totality of judges). Then there is that which proceeds by intensification and which attempts less to classify beings than to reach that which makes a being what he is, his essence – let's say his soul. The first form of abstraction does not exist in Bresson's work. His *Les Anges du péché* does not show us different 'types' of nun, his curé of Ambricourt is not The Priest – not even The Country Priest. He is not a type of country curé to which another type, the curé of Torcy forms a contrast. Hélène is not The Betrayed Mistress

Still: not a type – Mouchette.

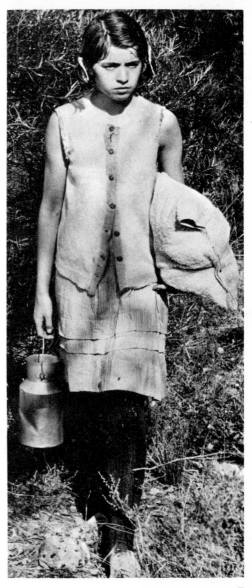

taking revenge. Fontaine is no more The Member of the Resistance than Michel is The Pickpocket (note that the film's title does not include the definite article).

What we find is the second type of abstraction, at least so far as the artist is capable of producing an equivalent. He can, in fact, choose to show by various devices the essence or soul of concrete reality, rather than its more or less chaotic workings. Instead of telling us everything about Lieutenant Fontaine and giving all the whys and wherefores of his actions in the Resistance, we are only given the bare essentials – though this does not stop him being perfectly individualised. Similarly, the pastoral life of the curé of Ambricourt is not described in detail and a close look will reveal a lot of omissions; this does not mean that any other priest cannot feel the brother of this man of God, even if in human terms he in no way resembles him. What I am saying is that this abstraction is not in any way pejorative: it does not result in the creation of bloodless people, bereft of character and personality, nor of mundane situations. The people we are shown are very strange, even though they have a universal relevance.

How does Bresson manage to give us only the essence of people and events without any feeling of thinness? Largely through a very precise choice of details, objects and accessories; through gestures charged with an extremely solid reality. André Bazin noted this in a well-known article on Bresson's style [reprinted later in this book]: 'All that was needed', he said, 'was the sound of a windscreen-wiper with a text by Diderot to produce a Racinian dialogue.' The sound of the windscreen-wiper has an equivalent in all Bresson's films, whether in the sound-track or the visuals. For example, the raking of the paths in the park during the curé's conversation with the Countess, or Joan of Arc's old shoes being consigned to the flames of her own funeral pyre. It is the stylistic arrangement of all these concrete details which ultimately delineates the soul of a character, a situation or a film. Bresson said somewhere that the director is a 'metteur en ordre'. He is isolating raw elements taken from real life and putting them together in a certain order. 'Like a painting,' he also said, 'a film should be made of relationships. To create is not to deform things nor to invent them, it is to give existing things new relationships.'

This aesthetic approach is analogous to that found in cubist or non-figurative painting, where the canvases are made of those rich, sensitive realities which are 'patches of colour arranged in a certain order', to take Maurice Denis's famous formula, or even of the elements of crude matter. Isn't the abstraction thus obtained of a different kind and less questionable in the end than that of those nineteenth century pictures representing 'Vengeance in pursuit of Crime', or 'Commerce and Industry crowning the Republic'? You will not find the equivalent of these works in Bresson, but, for example, in the Cayatte of *Justice est faite* or *Nous sommes tous des assassins*.

Bresson is quite conscious of his originality in this field. On the subject of *A Man Escaped* he said: 'I was hoping to make a film about objects which would at the same time have a soul. That is to say, to reach the latter through the former.' It is these objects presented in a certain order and in a certain style which reveal the soul. Bresson also said: 'I wanted all the factual details to be exact, but at the same time I tried to get beyond basic realism.' It is just the same in *The Trial of Joan of Arc* where objects and events keep all their weight as matter or reality: the chains, the ladder, the wood of the pyre, as well as the examination of Joan's virginity by

Still: coarse red wine – the priests of Torcy and Ambricourt in Diary of a Country Priest.

the women – yet the demands of style are never forgotten. The balance between abstraction and reality is as perfectly realised as in a painting by Vermeer.

Bresson's universe has evolved constantly in his increasingly controlled achievement of this balance. With *Les Anges* and *Les Dames*, abstraction definitely predominated. The simplification of story-line, decor and drama with the aim of making the essence clear did not occur without a certain complacency. We were meant to know that this simplicity was a style and that the style was not achieved without

effort. The objects or concrete details which were intended, as we have just said, to concentrate on themselves a certain coefficient of reality, were chosen more for their elegance than for their effectiveness. One would have thought this choice was made by the dialogue writers, Giraudoux or Cocteau, rather than by the director. The danger is that the result may be lack of substance, coldness, or an ethereal atmosphere. Too many things, too perfect, in too rarified an atmosphere.

With *Diary of a Country Priest* there is a complete change. Supreme elegance and a

slightly decadent refinement are no longer sought after to cover up the simplicity and bareness. Now coarse red wine, mud and vomit are there to remind us that even when men have reached the highest degrees of mysticism or the most subtle forms of art, they are never angels. In *A Man Escaped* the slop pails are emptied to music by Mozart, but this does not make the scene lose any of its 'realism', even if it gains new significance through the music.

Bresson as director is often reproached for extreme 'Jansenism'. He won't permit cheap display or vulgarity; he rejects spontaneity and the direct approach of daily life, but he does not go so far as to despise the humblest – even the lowest – things. It is true that under his direction they are never sordid; without appearing to touch them, he transfigures them. *Pickpocket* provides a particularly convincing illustration of this power. Nothing could be

Stills: A Man Escaped (*left*), Pickpocket. (*above*).

nastier or more mediocre than the character,
his immediate surroundings and his environment. Just think for a moment of the image a
Clouzot or an Autant-Lara could have made of
it. Yet, without obviously changing anything
in this mediocrity and apparent filthiness,
without expressionistic lighting or musical
effects, simply through the precision of directing

and acting, everything is turned inwards and
takes on a different meaning. Beyond the
surface, which is still as sordid as ever, one can
glimpse another dimension: that of the soul.

With reality as the starting point – happily
often a less mediocre reality – the rest of
Bresson's films are the same: it is always souls
that one finds. So it would now be appropriate
to examine how, through this universe where
abstraction and reality harmonise, these souls

are revealed through the characters which incarnate them.

From character to person

In the cinema as in the theatre and, by extension, even in 'the social comedy', one talks of characters. Basically the character is the likeness of a human being, the one which is exhibited to its fellow-creatures, the one which lives to be looked at. So for those who watch them, films are by definition peopled by characters. But within the worlds which are evoked, it is quite possible that for each other, too, they are characters. Such is frequently the case with comedy films which show human 'types' reduced to their outer skin; also with the sort of film known as 'commercial', where the superficial treatment is not susceptible to deeper psychological interpretation; it is even the case sometimes with those films whose ideological basis obliges them to admit to no human dimension other than that shown in society. By contrast, there are other works which claim to offer us something deeper, something beyond the social mask of their characters: either psychological 'characters' which are justified by their credibility and their inner cohesion, or 'symbols' charged with moral or metaphysical significance, or 'existences' of which a concrete description will enable one to grasp the sense or non-sense of human reality.

Bresson's characters show us none of these things. Certainly there is, particularly in the first two films, *Les Anges du péché* and *Les Dames du Bois de Boulogne*, some psychology of character. But apart from the fact that this diminishes progressively in importance in later films, it is significant to note that the fundamental traits – even in women – are not compassion or imagination, but will-power and lucidity, energy and obstinacy. Think of Anne-Marie and Thérèse, of Hélène, and even more

of Fontaine and the little curé of Ambricourt. The legionnaire on his motor-cycle makes no mistake when he says to the latter: 'You could have been one of us.' He is able to fight with the Countess and with Chantal 'soul for soul', with an obstinacy similar to that of Fontaine or of Chantal herself, who declares: 'I shall go to hell if I want to.' And even Michel the Pickpocket, who is apparently more passive, has a wild energy – 'I had made up my mind' – and a coldly calculating intelligence. Joan of Arc is tenacity itself. Not the obstinate peasant who refuses to give up her superstitious beliefs, but the clear-minded aristocrat who knows what she wants and why she wants it. But aren't the qualities of firmness and intelligence rather more of a moral than a psychological order?

Yet the characters which embody them are certainly not pure symbols or archetypes. Joan of Arc is not quite an Antigone, and Fontaine is only a Hamlet in reverse. Although they are not described in minute detail in a given situation in the neo-realist manner, they nonetheless attain, similarly, a certain area of meaning beyond psychology yet this side of symbolism. They open up a literally endless perspective on themselves, on the universe, even on the whole of existence. In fact there is always something fundamental and mysterious in them which escapes us. They emanate a sort of discomfort which means that they can never be truly sympathetic. The phenomenon of projection and identification has no part in them. They make us feel uncertain and uneasy. Where they are concerned, every ambiguity, if not equivocation, is possible. Who is Thérèse? Who is Hélène? Who are Chantal, the curé, Fontaine, Michel, Joan? 'The closer we get, the more they reveal themselves and the more obscure they become . . . instead of becoming clearer' (J. Arbois). In other words, they are more than

Still: the hero of Diary of a Country Priest.

12

characters, more than souls, they are people: 'the most perfect thing in nature' (S. Thomas), but also the most ineffable if it is true that in them is concentrated, in its almost pure state, the entire being of the universe.

This is why, even in their most extreme confidences, they never fundamentally reveal anything but their mystery – like God himself. Thus one can see them again and again without wearying of them, for they enrich but never satiate. Like Wisdom, 'They that eat me shall yet be hungry, and they that drink me shall yet be thirsty' (Ecclesiasticus XXIV, 21).

Stills: Joan of Arc; Au hasard, Balthazar.

This is even truer of the later films than of the early ones. In *Les Anges du péché* as in *Les Dames du Bois de Boulogne*, while there is a certain facility in the stylistic elegance, there is also something too mechanically intellectual and too obvious in the character make-up. Dare I say that the ambiguity has too little weight and one often brushes against the old analytical novel. In *Diary of a Country Priest*, however, the turning point has been reached and from there on the director, as though aware of Sartre's

famous criticism of Mauriac, avoids giving the impression that he knows everything about his characters on the pretext that he has created them. They are people whose ultimate secret is beyond him too.

Basically Bresson's style is an amalgam of strict but relatively simple means of achieving this end. There is always, for example, an increasing tendency towards inexpressiveness in the acting: anything which could be construed as direct communication through facial expression or gesture – in fact anything which might recall the theatre or even Elia Kazan's famous Actor's Studio – is avoided. In this way Bresson manages to achieve a genuineness which is finally more convincing than the impression produced by naturalistic acting. You would have to be a lawyer or prosecutor in a court of law before you could affect to believe (or be naïve enough to believe) in the facial expression of feeling, or the well-known sincere tone of voice. Instead, by asking his actors – more often than not non-professionals – not to 'act', or even, as has been said in comparison with standard technique, to 'act' or 'speak falsely', he endows the characters which they represent with a sort of aura of strangeness, as though one were dealing with people escaping in some way from our world. But this does not make them any less human, because he always takes special care to load them, their environment and the objects which surround them, with a sufficient weight of reality. Bresson even increasingly avoids giving too important a place to music, which would tend to increase dangerously the feeling of unreality; the music he chooses is intermittent and very pure: Mozart in *A Man Escaped* and Lully in *Pickpocket*. In *The Trial of Joan of Arc*, there is only a drum-roll at the beginning and the end, and the occasional distant sound of church bells. But more apparent than ever is the immobile mask and the neutral tone which give the film's heroine, over and above the social or moral aspects, an extraordinary resemblance to the other Jeanne – of *Pickpocket* – and even to Chantal in *Diary of a Country Priest*, just as one already existed between the curé, Lieutenant Fontaine and the pickpocket himself; this also endows the admirable historical text, to which Bresson wanted to be absolutely faithful, with a distinction and a spiritual relevance which realistic or expressive speech would have been unlikely to achieve to such a degree.

But if this strange tone seems to give an extra dimension to the character who uses it – and, taken in context, it is in fact the aesthetic equivalent of the mystery in the person – it also apparently makes communication, to which speech is normally devoted, not just problematical, but improbable. It is this further aspect of Bresson's universe which we must now consider.

From loneliness to communication

Many modern works, in the cinema and elsewhere, cultivate more or less successfully the theme of loneliness, preferably in a crowd, and produce variations which do not always manage to avoid a certain romantic complacency. By contrast, there is nothing less romantic than the loneliness of Bresson's characters. Theirs is not a sentimental attitude and it would be impossible to reveal the slightest complacency. On the contrary, they are fighting a constant, ruthless battle to reach each other by one means or another. They seem to know that their isolation is only apparent and that mysterious opportunities of meeting do exist, if one knows how to grasp them. They are like forest trees seen at eye-level, their smooth, stiff trunks well-spaced, always protected with bark, while underground, invisibly, their roots intermingle, and at the same time, high in the sky, their topmost branches lean towards one another in the hope that a breath of wind will enable them to touch. These people see each other, address each other, reproach each other, but even after they have been trying for a long time, communication is always a leap into the unknown, almost a miracle. Think of Anne-Marie and Thérèse in *Les Anges du péché*, of the curé and Chantal and the Countess, of Fontaine and Jost, of Michel and Jeanne. And the exchanges between Joan of Arc and her judges are more than a dialogue, they are a duel; yet a strange understanding is to be forged on the pyre between the executioners and the victim in the presence of the cross which they hold out to her and which she contemplates: an understanding in which all human contradictions are condensed and resolved.

Here again Bresson's style translates with perfect control a world in which neither communication nor loneliness are taken for granted, where, because of a fundamental discontinuity, meeting remains possible. In particular the spatio-temporal structure of all these films is also perfectly suited to this aspect. Thus we are always dealing with privileged areas, cut off from the rest of the world, as monasteries or prisons can be. We

Still: Thérèse (Jany Holt) in Les Anges du péché.

already have both in *Les Anges du péché*. In *Les Dames du Bois de Boulogne*, Agnès's and her mother's flat is a true prison to which Hélène has the key. In *Diary of a Country Priest* everyone remembers the castle and presbytery bars, and even more the 'prisoner of the Holy Agony'. *A Man Escaped, Pickpocket* and *The Trial of Joan of Arc* deal with prisons in the strictest sense.

Furthermore, these enclosed spaces which encompass the people who live in them do not have only one part: they are subdivided into juxtaposed cells, which are not without association but without links. You cannot go directly from one to another; there is always a space to be crossed, a staircase to go up or come down, corridors to be walked along. Think, for example, of the cells in the convent and of those in the prison in *Les Anges du péché*, of those in *A Man Escaped*, where the systematic absence of establishing shots serves to underline the partitioning. In *Les Dames du Bois de Boulogne*, the two flats perform the same function and the waterfall is a sort of neutral

Still: A Man Escaped.

cell where the meetings take place. The cars seem like moving cells which each character takes with him and in which he is separated from the others, even if only by a window. Even the famous sequence of the lift and the staircase becomes profoundly significant when seen from this angle. So does the pickpocket's lonely room, simultaneously connected with and separated from the outside world by a sordid staircase. But it is with *The Trial of Joan of Arc* that the cellular universe reaches its final paroxysm: here the whole film is set in the rooms of the Château de Rouen which have been turned into a prison.

How can one help thinking of the space which Bresson, the erstwhile painter, may have meditated upon, the space of cubist paintings, where one is dealing not with an unique perspective which binds together and unifies everything but with a partitioning of facets which are entangled with each other without intermingling because they are always separated by rigid edges. But here the intervention of a temporal dimension allows for a more complete orchestration of discontinuity. In the first place, this is because time in the film is shown as being firmly bounded by a beginning and an end, with no extension into an hypothetical future. What Thérèse or Michel are going to do at the end of *Les Anges du péché* and *Pickpocket* or what Fontaine will do after his escape, is of no interest to us. In the other films, death definitively closes off the flow of time, even though it may open up new horizons. Moreover, this enclosed time itself is made up of a succession – almost a juxtaposition – of moments with no quality of duration. For instance, in *Les Dames du Bois de Boulogne*, the fade-outs are not sufficient to bind together the separate moments: the taxi, Hélène and Jean, Hélène alone, Madame D's cabaret, the waterfall . . . Nor is there more flowing duration in *A Man Escaped*. The escape plan which should unite everything in fact only justifies each element. 'The door had to open', says Fontaine, 'I had no plans beyond that', and André Bazin comments: 'His fate and his liberty are sufficient to each moment, indeed to each shot.' *Pickpocket* is no different: its extremely fragmented outline, with unusually abrupt cuts and ellipses, has often surprised and disconcerted both spectators and critics. And in *Diary of a Country Priest*, Bresson has managed to edit out entire sequences without causing any irritation. Everyone knows that the number of Stations of the Cross, which has been fixed at fourteen, is purely arbitrary. It can be done validly with one small cross. The whole of Bresson's film is that cross which summarises it as much as ends it. And in *The Trial of Joan of Arc*, each scene, each interrogation, even each question and answer could be self-sufficient, at least to the extent that the whole film is latent in each exchange.

The very striking discontinuity of space and time in Bresson's universe and the loneliness of the characters which it expresses, seems to be supported by the hidden inclusion of everything in each part and of everyone in each person. Because of this, neither loneliness nor communication is taken for granted, and both create problems. Even so, it has been pointed out that the stress moves from the former towards the latter from one film to the next, from *Les Anges du péché* to *The Trial of Joan of Arc*. Bresson's people, we were saying, are like forest trees side by side, seeming not to notice that their roots intermingle, but stretching their branches across the space towards each other in order to make contact when a chance breath of wind helps them. This parallel is valid from *Les Anges du péché* to *The Trial of Joan of Arc*, but a fundamental fellowship seems to become more apparent: roots bare themselves and the wind blows more often.

Les Anges du péché is summed up in Anne-Marie's and Thérèse's attempt to communicate. Failures and pseudo-successes follow each other, but each stays in her prison – a prison of hate or of self-sufficiency. The only things which can close the gap are Anne-Marie's sacrifice and death: Thérèse leaves the convent which has been her prison and voluntarily enters the prison which will prove a true convent for her, the place where she regains her inner freedom. The four characters in *Les Dames du Bois de Boulogne* are no less shut up in themselves, and the attempt by one woman to reunite the other two is seen by her as a method of separating them even further. Agnès's death is apparently a success, but is in fact a drastic failure. The curé, though trying with all his might to communicate, finds his own loneliness forming a constant barrier between him and the loneliness of others. He makes souls close up; Chantal here wears the same mask as Maria Casarès in the previous film. In the last resort, he with his humility is as impotent as Anne-Marie with her pride. Still, we do find here, unexpectedly, souls which open up: the

Countess, Séraphita, Dufréty's friend, and perhaps Chantal herself . . .

But it is above all in *A Man Escaped* that isolation – I mean real isolation within apparent communication – gives way to solitude – apparent isolation where there is real communication. Fontaine in his cell is apparently alone; in reality, in truth, he is not alone. The prison is a world of communication, even of communion. If he escapes, it will be thanks to all those who surround him: the prayers of some, the advice of others, and the experience of all. The sign of this real communion in apparent solitude is the music from Mozart's Mass, heard each time they walk round the yard with their slop pails. People have seen life, liberty and God in this music. I see all those, but also unity, brotherhood, and communion. The music does not express the rather facile side to brotherhood, 'the too human human', as seen by De Sica, but perhaps it has greater depth. If Fontaine had held out his hand to Jost in the first place, like a rather stupid big brother, instead of originally considering killing him – yes, killing him – their community in adventure would certainly not have been so complete. Bresson explained this aspect in an interview: 'Fontaine finally holds out his hand to Jost in spite of himself, not to perform an act of generosity – quite the contrary – but because of that fellowship which binds us to each other, without our knowledge (and whether we want it or not) across life's partitions, as across the partitions of Montluc prison. It is chance which leads Jost into Fontaine's cell, or the wind which bloweth where it listeth . . .' In Bresson's work there are always partitions, but thanks to human energy and the mysterious breath which animates them, these partitions seem to become less hermetically sealed.

Like *A Man Escaped*, *Pickpocket* is also a story of communication, but it begins with one of the most impenetrable cases of loneliness ever shown on the screen. Of all Bresson's characters, this one is certainly the most of an 'outsider' – and they all are to a greater or lesser degree. He is isolated by his vice even among his equals. 'He is alone with them, alone in the crowd, happy. Alone with his hands' (Jean Collet). The theme of the hands has a role here which is antithetical to that in *A Man Escaped*. While the Lieutenant uses his to win his liberty, to get rid of his handcuffs and communicate with others, the diabolical dexterity of Michel's hands, 'the marvellous beating of wings' (René Guyonnet) ultimately serves only to rebuild the enclosed space, all-enveloping and lonely, of which he is the sovereign lord, because he is alone there: this situation could only end with handcuffs and prison. But a series of apparently unconnected meetings – of the mother, the woman and the child – will one day quite suddenly release him from his inner prison. Finally he discovers that someone else besides himself exists, and, through the bars which still cut him off from her, he hugs this unique person whose kiss reconciles him with the universe.

This is a happy ending which in another context could have been melodramatic, but here, although surrounded by apparent coherence, everything is so strange, so obviously predetermined by external forces, that one is obliged to accept it like the rest. Still, perhaps it would be a good thing to analyse this type of justification and see how those things which are of man and those which are beyond him work in this special universe.

From immanence to transcendence

So far it has been impossible to avoid referring constantly to an invisible dimension which can be felt in each character and even more strongly in their connections with each other. But this dimension is not on the same plane or even in direct extension of the others. Trans-

Still: Jeanne and Michel in Pickpocket.

cendence here is only an additional element which intervenes from outside by some means or other. We are dealing with immanent transcendence, or even, one might say, with radical invisibility. For the invisible world remains invisible, or rather appears only as invisible. When Bresson was offered a four millimetre cross to distinguish the priest in *A Man Escaped*, he said: 'I'm afraid it may be a bit big.' This is not timidity and fear of allowing too much importance to the Absolute. On the contrary, it is concern that it should not become relative, not just have a place among

other things, when it should be everything, the soul of everything. And it turns out that, far from being obscured by so much caution, the mysterious presence of the 'wind which bloweth where it listeth,' becomes all the more hauntingly irrefutable by remaining impalpable. So much so that one may well wonder whether the word God is ever spoken in any of the films, even *Les Anges du péché* or *Diary of a Country Priest*. It is there like the other side of the world, or rather like the real place of which we only know the other side, what André Bazin nicely terms *le côté pile de la face de Dieu* (the tails side of the face of God). It is situated in discontinuity, in the void we were talking about earlier. In other words, it is confused with freedom, for each free action seems a leap across this void, a true miracle. The Absolute does not influence men in the way that one thing acts upon another. It is simply at the heart of their freedom – its soul. On the subject of *A Man Escaped*, Bresson said: 'I want to show this miracle: an invisible hand on the prison directing events and making something succeed for one person and not for another . . .' An invisible hand which never acts except by the hand of Fontaine, by that obstinate hand that makes tools and forces doors. 'Help yourself,' said the original title of the film. There is even an invisible hand in *Diary of a Country Priest*, in *Les Anges*, in *Les Dames*, in *Pickpocket*, and of course in *The Trial of Joan of Arc*. It is this which made Henri Agel write: 'Bresson, like Pascal and the true poets, lifts the moment from its temporal framework and transfigures it into a piece of eternity.'

How does this eternity appear, while remaining invisible? Mainly through the inexpressiveness of faces and through death. By expressing nothing, the masks express precisely that which is beyond expression. Think of the faces of Thérèse, Hélène, Chantal, Michel, Joan . . . The whole point is that behind these inexpressive faces lies death. Jacques Prévert wrote: 'how vague, inconsistent and disturbing a live face would seem to us if there was not a death mask inside it'. But even if Bresson's characters do not always see their own death, they have no difficulty in seeing death around them and in seeing in it the sign and the gate to the beyond. In *Les Anges*, Thérèse's conversion takes place between the murder of her lover and Anne-Marie's death. In *The Diary of a Country Priest* there is the baby's death, the

Countess's, the doctor's and finally the curé's. Even *Les Dames* loses all its point if one does not admit Agnès's death at the end of the film. In *Pickpocket* the death and burial of the mother are the episodes which appear to correspond to an experience peculiar to Bresson; they are at the centre of Michel's drama, and will be the point of departure for his final evolution. 'I believed in God for three minutes,' he says to Jeanne. But when you've believed like that for a moment, it goes on for ever. That's why this 'outsider' in contrast to Camus's (although he, too, sees his mother die) will receive grace and his diabolical hands will be purified.

But it is with *The Trial of Joan of Arc* that death takes on its true face of eternity, that of sacrifice, foreshadowed in *Diary of a Country Priest*. Joan, in spite of her courage in armed combat and even in the more terrifying battle of words, is afraid of death and in particular of death by fire: she thinks her virgin body has not merited this ultimate purification. It is really only at the end, when there can be no more hope of any other sort of liberation, that she will finally agree to see in it the predestined means of meeting Him whose Voices have never deceived her. The shots of the pyre which end the film translate with a simplicity and beauty rarely attained in other sacred art this accession through death to eternal life. This very pure body literally fades away into the sky and only a half-burnt stake is left to mark for the people who remain one of those mysterious points in time when the paths of history and eternity have crossed.

Yet again, in Bresson's work, it is never one thing sacrificed to another, neither history to eternity, nor grace to freedom. The two mysteriously coexist, or rather interpenetrate, rather as the soul and body do. It is significant that Bresson hesitated a long time between two titles for the film which eventually became *A Man Escaped*: '*Le vent souffle où il veut* . . . –

The wind bloweth where it listeth' and 'Aide-toi – Help yourself . . .' ('heaven will help you' is understood). This is why a partial study of Bresson's universe can always produce differing interpretations. For example, one could perfectly well refuse to see in it anything but man, his will and his history. In that case, it would be stressed that decisions and events are formed by minds and resolute spirits. If you are a prisoner, you are told, use your brain and your hands. Your freedom lies in your human hands. And if your companion fails, although he may be 'courage itself', it's because he didn't reflect for long enough. But if you are an unfortunate, lonely and despairing priest, fight yourself with all your strength, fight the evil that is in you and around you. Fight without hope or logic, just for the beauty of the gesture, just as, on a different plane, a young Legionnaire does. Then, even if God remains silent, you will attain peace. If, on the other hand, you are what society calls a thief, don't think yourself marked with some indelible blemish which will be either your shame or your pride, but know that you yourself have chosen to be like that. All you must do is simply look out for other things in you and around you, other forces which surround you and which can be as strong, if you wish, as your vice: the dying look of your mother; the child you find by the way; the woman you have not yet been able to see. It is there that your freedom lies. In you and around you, in your human universe. If, however, you have given all your strength to the service of your country and your enemies have defeated you and have you in their power, then renounce none of your ideals, die in hope, for the example of your sacrifice may perhaps serve your cause better than your most outstanding actions would have done.

Why, then, seek grace in a world where prisoners can attain freedom simply by brute force; where a young priest finds peace by fighting despair alone; where a proud thief ends by accepting a humble form of communication with his fellow creatures, after very subtle but very definite and profound preparation; where a heroine finally sacrifices herself without showing weakness because she has faith in the future? Why seek grace? Because, if you look more closely, grace is there, powerful even while invisible. In fact there is nothing but grace – its sovereign omnipotence obscures everything else. Because 'the wind bloweth where it listeth', one prisoner will escape and another will be killed; one thief will recant, another will die in sin; one priest will retain a strong and unfailing hope, another will know the depths of complete moral and spiritual abandonment. Why? Doubtless one can provide vague human reasons, but they are always insufficient, and in the end only God knows. 'All is grace', but that is why nothing is freedom. Should we not say of those who think they can escape from its grasp – of Chantal in *Diary of a Country Priest*, the executioners in *A Man Escaped* and *The Trial of Joan of Arc*, and even more of Hélène in *Les Dames* – that they are literally 'graceless' in the manner of certain Racinian characters (this is not the first time that the relationship between Bresson and Racine has been underlined), that they are Christians without grace. In other words, to the Jansenism that Bresson is so often accused of in his direction, he adds an undeniably Jansenist way of thinking.

The fact that two such contradictory interpretations can reasonably be upheld at the same time shows only one thing: we are dealing, as Pascal would say, with two faces of the same truth. Instead of choosing, then, we must agree that in Bresson's universe 'all is grace' but simultaneously 'all is freedom'. No formula could be more orthodox if the Doctor of grace, St. Augustine, is to be believed: '. . . as the law is not made void but established through

23

faith, since faith procures the grace whereby the law is fulfilled, so the freedom of the will is not made void through grace, but rather is thereby established . . .' ('*De spiritu et littera*', XXX, 52). Seen in this light, it is perhaps significant that it has proved possible to make the Jeanne of *Pickpocket* simultaneously a symbol of grace and of freedom. When she embraces Michel through the prison bars, she is grace bringing freedom.

These are some of the aspects of Bresson's universe which seem essential. Although he saw the light almost twenty years ago – a relatively long time in the brief history of the cinema – one cannot fail to be struck by his youthfulness. While the old guard of the cinema persist in repeating endlessly the old formulae on which their youthful success was based – when they are not trying, with touching willingness to please, to borrow the trappings of the latest fashions from the more turbulent of their young disciples – Bresson, with an imperturbable disregard for the cinema around him, has only to be himself to gain quite naturally a place in the vanguard – the only valid section – of what has been too complacently called the New Wave. The films of Alain Resnais, of Truffaut, of Chris Marker or of Agnès Varda, whatever their inner differences may be, are all involved in the same search as Bresson.

The superseding of analytical psychology, which had scarcely evolved since Paul Bourget; the extreme importance given to the text and its dissonances with the picture; the entirely new evaluation of the different forms of temporality; the recognised value of empty space and absence; a certain hieratic quality in the acting, the rejection of theatrical performances and traditional dramatisation, not to mention the all too well known 'distanciation': all these constitute, even more than the thematic element, a common climate which is that of the true modern cinema. If Bresson can be seen as the precursor, chronologically, and if the whole younger generation respects him because of this, he is not reduced as a result to the honorary role of venerable ancestor; far from it, he remains a contemporary and an equal. Besides, in our epoch of speeded up history, one no longer bows to age, but only to mastery.

Still: Mouchette.

24

LES ANGES DU PECHE

RAYMOND DURGNAT

Many directors, like Carl Dreyer, gradually find themselves through their works. Others, notably in Hollywood, gradually lose themselves. Others again, including Bresson, ceaselessly transpose and refine a vision almost mature in their first feature.

Anne-Marie (Renée Faure) is a girl of good family who attaches herself to the Sisters of Bethany, a Dominican order devoted to the rescue and rehabilitation of women with criminal records. Almost too high-spirited and strong-willed, she is seized with a particular concern for one Thérèse (Jany Holt), whose response is hatred. Liberated, Thérèse shoots the man on whose behalf she was unjustly imprisoned, and returns for refuge to the convent, to the joy of Anne-Marie, who is ignorant of her real motives. Sensing that the girl's weak point is pride, Thérèse flatters her, and lures her into denouncing the sub-Prioress for excessive love of a cat, and the Sisters for hypocritically fawning on it too. Refusing penance (to kiss the feet of all the nuns), she is expelled. But, humbly, she creeps in each night to pray at the grave of Father Lataste, the Order's founder. Caught in a downpour, she falls ill, and is nursed by Thérèse, whom she dissuades from returning to her disorderly existence. Dying, she is unable to pronounce her vows. Thérèse speaks them for her, and is led, manacled, from the convent, past the nuns, to the last of whom she murmurs: 'A bientôt ...'

The issue of Thérèse's salvation is counterpointed against the subtler issue of Anne-Marie's. The film is a study of, in a sense, twin souls: of two rebels finding peace through each other and through the system, a system which needs its rebels, but no more than they need it. Thérèse's machinations aim, not simply at the expulsion of Anne-Marie, but via some unconscious diabolism, at her damnation, through pride – that aggressive vehemence in one's subjective conscience which Protestantism may applaud but which Catholicism certainly does not. The film is constructed around intimations of that very un-Protestant notion of 'transferability of merit': the pure soul offers itself as an atoning scapegoat for the evil one – a notion which fascinates Mauriac and other French Catholics, perhaps because of the challenge it poses to purely 'psychological' views of salvation.

That Anne-Marie shares Thérèse's contrariness is hinted in two early scenes. Her initial refusal to burn the photographs of her family, by way of worldly renunciation, is presented in terms of a refusal which disappoints a not-too-intolerant Sister. And her decision to burn them is presented in terms of its painful effect on her worldly mother. Does Bresson twice portray loyalty and sacrifice, as hurtful wilfulness, only to maintain ambiguity and suspense? Or does this ambiguity express something real in his heroine?

For Bardèche and Brasillach, the story is 'a matter less of God, than of domination and sacrifice'. From this angle, it closely parallels Bresson's next film, Les Dames du Bois de Boulogne, a tale of profane revenge transcended by acceptance. There, a lady transforms a

25

sinner, to revenge herself on a man; here, a lady converts a sinner also, perhaps, as a mere sublimation of sadism. The religious film has as its cachet of artistic authenticity that, from a lay angle, it makes an even more disturbing kind of sense. It is tragic rather than cynical, and all the more movingly pessimistic in that the characters, as they are, have anyway no real path to happiness. Nor, even from a non-believer's angle, is it possible not to admire Anne-Marie's attempts to obliterate her personality among those of the other nuns.

Pride and matching solitude are perennial

Stills: Les Anges du péché.

Bresson themes. In Dreyer, in Bergman, there is a certain sociability in cruelty, as well as in love; they are humanist in their sense of flesh, of frustrations, of worldly happiness and will. Bresson's is altogether a non-humanist vision. His is a cinema of vocations, expressed either as environments which enfold and transform (convent, prison) or ways of life which isolate (a priest's, a pickpocket's, a donkey's). His first film is a film of two prisons: prison, and convent. It may not be accidental that Bresson's

26

career begins with two studies in feminine ascendancies and proceeds to studies of lonely male victims. But he is too aloof and alive to be caught in any particular psychological posture; *Mouchette* closes the circle. That soft, grey, Bresson light no more than slightly camouflages the fact that his victims and angels have wills of marble, hard enough to damn themselves, were they not saved by – something... At the same time, the grey light reduces the faces to a grey paste, to, as it were, the ectoplasm of the Holy Spirit, to accidental forms of an un-differentiated divinity. Whence, perhaps, the celebrated exchange in a *Cinéma 63* symposium on Bresson:

'There aren't any sympathetic female characters in Bresson –'
'There aren't any sympathetic characters in Bresson!'
'Are there any characters in Bresson?'

Les Anges du péché isn't what to Protestant eyes it might suggest, the story of Anne-Marie versus the system *qua* system. Anne-Marie is no Joan of Arc, with her direct hot line to God, by-passing the Papal switchboard. She is

sustained, in her exile, by her prayers at the grave of the Order's founder (subsequently canonised), a situation suggestive of prayers to saints. The testy sub-Prioress is matched by a wise Prioress. If Anne-Marie is of those violent ones who take the kingdom of Heaven by force (Matthew, IX, 12), her force is also that of self-submission. Bresson gives his special twist to the truism that the ways of Providence are too strange for anyone to understand, that we can do no more than strive to purify ourselves in response to God's initiatives. Abjuring the Calvinist stress on positive, righteous action,

Stills: Above – at the grave of the Order's founder. Right – the sisters at work.

Bresson attains his curious, almost cold, air of passivity, of aloofness matching anguish; thus, too, he can take that Calvinist text, 'The wind bloweth where it listeth', for *Un Condamné à mort s'est echappé*, and give it a Jesuit, rather than a Calvinist, meaning (i.e. the spirit inspires a man without revelation).

Un-Protestant also is Bresson's profound respect for convent life, for its rituals, its ceremonies (the nuns drawing texts, by lot, to provide their annual motto), the 'fraternal corrections', the gestures of penitence – all of which lose all exoticism, all picturesquerie, and assume their functional beauty. He catches the grace of dedicated practicality, and the matter-of-factness of sincere ceremony. The two fuse, as the film's climax is carried almost entirely by the verbal formulas of initiation into the Order. The sense of convent life, its spirit and gestures, is very far from being documentary, and is perhaps the film's strongest claim to greatness.

Bresson elides the sensationalism offered by the story's nun-vice confrontation (one may nonetheless regret even the Prioress's brief telephone conversation: 'Is it the driver I asked for, the big one, who is devoted to us?... Edward will be our driver. He's an ex-boxer.'). Thérèse's killing of her man is all the more ruthless for its reticence. She rings a bell, waits by a wall. Steps sound, the door opens, its light frames Thérèse. A man's voice says, '*C'est toi. Bonjour.*' '*Bonjour*', she replies, and fires three shots. The terseness out-Hawks Hawks; the scene moves so fast that it loses all sense of motion. The only sensuous touches concern emblems of death and liberation:

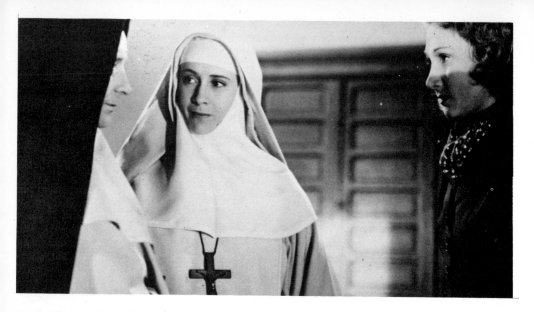

handcuffs locked on Thérèse's wrist, and the rain slapping Anne-Marie's white face.

Bresson's selectivity results from his marked hierarchy of values, and relates him to a classical tradition. For a romantic tradition, great art strives to lyricise as many threads as possible of life's rich pattern, e.g. Shakespeare has as many facets as he has readers. But if romanticism accumulates, classicism excludes. If romanticism favours the lyric poem, classicism favours the apothegm, the *pensée*. If romanticism seeks general insights through highly individualised particulars, classicism often eschews the individual, seeking the central conflicts with general truths. In a classical approach to movies the reason for a scene moulds the scene (in a romantic approach, the scene explodes in all directions; it may gain many details, but each detail bears less weight). To the Shakespeare-Dickens-Joyce line of romantic realism, we may oppose that of Racine-Pascal-Gide. In Racine,

profane passions have a noon-day heat; Bresson writes at dusk. And he is almost feline in his ambiguity as between Racine's Jansenism and Corneille's orthodox conception of free will.

Most surprising, perhaps, is the Bressonisation, by a then 'unknown' director, of Giraudoux's dialogue. The playwright's gift for philosophical, rather than for psychological drama, already suited Bresson's vision of providence overriding psychology, but his abundance of phrases had to be reduced to bedrock terseness, his gracefulness made ascetic. Already Bresson detheatricalises drama without loss of intensity. If Renée Faure's dewy petulance too often belies her nun's mask, the effect does not destroy the deeper truth. In the prison scenes, Jany Holt's ferocity leads the mind tantalisingly beyond Bresson's range. As the Prioress, Sylvie doesn't even acknowledge the McCareyesque sentimentalities into which the role would lead less supply firm a mind.

Bresson's asceticism exacerbates, rather than obliterates, nuance. 'Painting taught me that one shouldn't make beautiful pictures, but necessary pictures. Plastically. One must sculpt the idea in a face by light and shade.' But, 'What I seek is not so much expression by gesture, word or mime, as expression by the rhythm and combinations of images, by their position, relationship and number.' The apparent contra-diction is really a matter of complementarity; and the parallel with Eisenstein, who popular-ised montage while also intensifying the separate image, reminds one that Bresson's, like Godard's, is a cinema of montage, in the sense of depending on juxtaposition and omission, on images assuming the abstraction of the words which overlay them. That Bresson's is a world of essence without accidents, Godard's one of accidents without essence, doesn't alter the case. Bresson, before Godard, had the courage to *read aloud*; Godard simply geared Bresson's style to headline speed rather than prayerbook

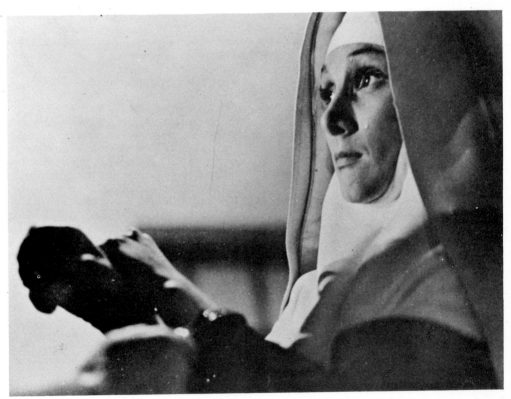

calm. Godard crossed his i's and dotted his t's.

Les Anges du péché still stands on the brink of this transformation. There is some truth in the criticism that 'what touches the clash of consciences and the heart's secrets is often expressed by rather crude means: prayers in monologue, melodramatic scenes; and then that dying nun looks rather too healthy, is rather too pretty with her round cheeks and plucked eyebrows...Nonetheless,...he has opened the invisible door...' The Fascist opinions of Bardèche and Brassilach are not irrelevant to a movie well suited to the Vichy clericalism of its time, and the film has not outgrown a moral glibness which Bresson, perhaps, accepts and exploits, without really subscribing to it, but which he doesn't repudiate until *Pickpocket*. The nunnery-underworld is, by higher Christian standards, as glib as, fortunately, it is peripheral. At least the nunnery has its apple of discord, the cat (a malevolent counterpart of Balthazar?). Nor need we give Bresson the benefit of our doubt whether the relationship between the highborn Anne-Marie and the lowborn Thérèse implies a social paternalism. And Bresson's keen eye for the functional beauty of convent life only sharpens the temptation to reverse its terms: the convent, however fine its purpose and pure its joys, is, in some respects, an idealistic, an idealised, an ideal, Fascist, or, if you prefer, a Platonic republic. Deprived of autonomy, the individual must make the general will his own; his spirit must become as white and flat as the cell walls, exposed, scrubbed, for God's perpetual inspection.

Yet one can subscribe to something in the sense of Henri Agel's remark on the film's flaws: 'A spectator at the Ciné-Club recently accused the film of being "glycerine". Glycerine, if you like, *Les Anges du péché*, but in how Surrealist a manner!'

From a Surrealist, or even a humanist angle, Bresson's world is, of course, one of self-mutilation, redeemed less by its moral heroism than by its tragic intensity. (Hence Bresson's one popular success is a resistance story, not overtly religious.) This bleakness reflects, perhaps, a fallen world, in which instinct is blighted, frostbitten, congealed, by sin and guilt, and can never quite reflect the Creator's glory, even in transcendence. Devotion apart, Bresson's characters are left with – not quite suicide, not quite hatred, but – obstinacy, in rejection, as in acceptance (only grace can ease their passage from one to the other). The light that spiritualises the faces also becomes a dark cold mist, softening, drowning fields and streets. Bresson's first two films may be battles between women, but one can't imagine him catching the lay passions of, say, *Mädchen In Uniform;* nor can one imagine him doing other than reverse the tragic force of Gide's 'Strait is The Gate'.

Where Dreyer's images are solid, sculptural, exterior, Bresson's grey shades seem almost interior; imprints on the emulsions of a mind. Bazin remarked on Bresson's tendency to abstraction. But abstract can mean, variously, 'without physical form' (an abstract idea), or 'without mental content' (an abstract painting). And one should, perhaps, speak not of abstraction, but of purity, of a will to exclusion, enabling him to pioneer the anti-rhetoric, the negativism, of Godard, of Antonioni, of Warhol, of Dwoskin. At the end of *L'Eclisse*, the characters disappear behind the crossroads, as the country priest behind the cross. Both Bresson's film and Warhol's *Harlot* venture into the world behind the image – Warhol's with joyous nihilism, revealing the world of the film's making, Bresson's, going through the 'invisible door'. And, surely, the slyly inserted hand of Bresson's *Pickpocket* is echoed in the insinuated fingers of Zelda, *Alone*, in Dwoskin's film.

LES DAMES DU BOIS DE BOULOGNE

DANIEL MILLAR

Anyone who first came across Bresson in the 'fifties will have noted common characteristics in *Journal*, *Condamné* and *Pickpocket*: a deep exploration of an isolated man's spiritual state through intense study of his face and hands, attitudes and movements, and through his narrating, commenting interior monologue; a stress on routine and confinement, in which may flower a paradoxical freedom; drab clothes and stark, bare settings, filmed strictly on location, with little or no studio work; a low-key, matt, realistic photographic style (L.-H. Burel); a sense of ritual, either overtly religious or apparently secular, emphasised sparingly by music; a reticently indirect treatment of sex and of emotion generally; a predominance of non-professional actors.

Later admirers who know *Balthazar* and *Mouchette* best may have a slightly different set of associations: the young girl as victim; the coarse, harsh rural setting, with its head-on personal conflicts, greed and meanness, heavy drinking, cruelty to animals and to humans; ironically sunny, high-key photography (Ghislain Cloquet) with a vivid feeling of texture and a high proportion of visually convincing night scenes; an extremely elliptical manner in both image and sound editing, and in narrative, with no clues from any commentary and few from the sparse dialogue, permitting an expansion of material included and span of time covered; strict use of non-actors.

Les Dames will not fit into either slot. Bazin subtly grouped it with *Journal* as a novel species of adaptation, while noting that the 'happy few' who had admired *Les Dames* were puzzled and disappointed by *Journal*. Indeed, most of Bresson's films, like most films, are adapted from literary, at least printed, originals. But only in the case of *Les Dames* has the adaptation itself been a subject of misunderstanding and a topic of controversy.

The source in Diderot's '*Jacques le fataliste*' is the tale of the Marquise de la Pommeraye and the Marquis des Arcis, told by the hostess and running, with frequent interruptions and comments by Jacques, his Master and Diderot himself, to about fifty pages. It comprises a couple of dozen short scenes, many in dramatic form, detailing the motivation and mechanics of Mme de la Pommeraye's revenge on her ex-lover. She is present in literally every scene from the time she discovers that he no longer loves her until, nearly a year later, her revelation on the day after his wedding that he has married a whore. Except for the meeting in the Jardin du Roi, every scene up to the denouement takes place at her house; and the girl, Mlle d'Aisnon, has in all only three or four lines of dialogue before she becomes Mme des Arcis. Then, with the switch of location to the Marquis's house, she suddenly becomes loquacious and pleads her case for a whole page – though, unlike Agnès her counterpart in the film, she has had a fortnight to recover from her fainting, and anyway M. des Arcis has already decided to forgive her.

Clearly Bresson did not have recourse to Cocteau as dialoguist in order to select from or even modernise Diderot – it was hardly beyond

33

his powers to make the adaptation from Diderot's '*Je vous avouerai que l'histoire de votre coeur est mot à mot l'histoire du mien. Tous ce que vous êtes dit, je me le suis dit; mais je me taisais, je souffrais, et je ne sais quand j'aurais eu le courage de parler*' to Cocteau's version: '*L'histoire de votre coeur est mot pour mot la triste histoire du mien. Tout ce que vous êtes dit, je me le suis dit. Je me taisais, je souffrais, je n'osais pas vous en ouvrir la bouche. Quelle leçon*'. Though the selections and changes are sometimes more thorough-going, there are no fewer than ten separate scenes of duologue involving Hélène and Jean, each one closely related to an original in Diderot.

It is Agnès, of course, who requires all the additional dialogue to go with the extra scenes invented for her in Bresson's scenario – no less than six with her mother, two extended meetings with Jean and also two with Hélène, plus both her encounters with the stage-door johnnies, not to mention two quite long dances, the composer's concern rather than Cocteau's. For Agnès has to be transformed from passive but complaisant instrument of revenge to relatively innocent victim – her descendants are Jeanne in *Pickpocket* and even Mouchette, not the 'bad girl' like Chantal in *Le Journal* who is, even in looks, the spiritual daughter of Hélène. But, though by no means Diderot's veteran of a decade as a whore, Agnès is surely not as virginal as her saintly namesake. Bresson is quite sufficiently explicit within the conventions of the 'forties and reserves his ellipses for a more delicate issue, her involvement in the intrigue. The two most notable ellipses are in the two encounters by the Cascade in the Bois de Boulogne. The dissolve from Agnès's face as Jean first sees it to the discussion afterwards between Jean and Hélène prevents our discovering how Hélène manages to make the meeting seem spontaneous without seriously arousing Agnès's suspicions. Again, at the meeting between Agnès and Jean alone, the noise of the waterfall actually drowns his presumably eloquent words even before the dissolve to her in the car later on, so that we cannot imagine how he has successfully managed to persuade her to run off with him (to the Riviera?) without even guessing at the contents of her unread letter. Such seemingly dialogue problems are boldly solved by Bresson with a couple of strokes from the editor's china-clay pencil.

Probably the additions and the changes to Agnès's character and the transposition from 1774 to 1944 have caused less difficulty than the mixture of conventions. For instance, it is easy enough to 'read' the cinematic meaning of Agnès's old raincoat thrown over her scanty black dance costume (Démy gives it exactly the same tarty significance, though a lighter tone, in his *hommage*, *Lola*) and the street-walker overtones of the coat persist, less strongly, through the film. Similarly, the cigarette smoke deliberately blown in her face by her dancing-partner reduces her metaphorically to the level of a taxi-dancer – and her resentment recognises the measure of truth in the insult. But these clearly iconographic elements co-exist, in the same scenes, with the most remarkably nun-like (because hooded) of Hélène's many long, black dresses – the length is justified by the evening, as in preceding scenes, but the startling close-up of her smoking her only cigarette in the whole film almost makes us forget to ask how she manages socially to go to a night-club alone. And soon enough we are again puzzled, or delighted, with the link between the pseudo-American style of the club and the dance, and the Chicagoesque associations of Hélène's '*Suivez cette voiture!*' to her chauffeur, amid the murky streetlights

Still: the meeting by the Cascade – Jean (Paul Bernard) and Agnès (Elina Labourdette).

and big, black cars. Has Hélène become a moral G-man or possibly – as her '*Je me vengerai*' in the preceding scene suggests – a moral Mafiosa? More simply, do her perpetually floor-length black dresses imply widowhood (as in Diderot), or mourning for Jean's lost love, or simply that she is a *grande dame* of a special timeless breed?

In fact, most of Bresson's films exist in a timeless world even when, as in *Condamné* or *Jeanne d'Arc*, they are rooted in a precise year. So Hélène is timeless not only in relation to the social world but also to the other characters. Maria Casarès was just twenty-one when the film was made; but Hélène, usually bejewelled herself, snatches away Agnès's earrings with a sarcastic '*Est-ce de votre âge de porter des bijoux de cette valeur?*'. Like the idea of the

Still: Hélène (Maria Casarès).

mother and daughter of indistinguishable age in Godard's *Les Carabiniers*, the convention can be accepted or simply ignored, but not usefully questioned. The only sequences which are firmly fixed in the mid-'forties, by the crowd extras, are the wedding and reception. Otherwise, if Bresson had made the film now, rather than a quarter-century ago, the differences would presumably be less in such details than in casting.

The question of acting or of non-acting is unavoidable, particularly with *Les Dames*, where Bresson used professional actors in all principal roles for the last time. It seems likely that it was precisely the problems of working with professionals on *Les Dames* which led to their drastic reduction in *Journal* and total exclusion thereafter. But knowing that Bresson had rows with Maria Casarès does not affect interpretation or evaluation. Indeed her performance is practically the only aspect of the film to be universally admired, and the reason for its success may be hinted at in Godard's interview question (May 1966): 'Would it interest you, for example, to make a film about an actor? And if you had it to make, how would you make it? I mean a film on the act of playing.' *Les Dames* was already that film. Though Hélène must spend vast tracts of her time alone – and this is a large part of her tragedy – we catch only the briefest glimpses of her *temps-mort*, perhaps as she is petting her little white dog; nearly always we see her acting a role – with Jean, with Agnès, with Mme D., with Jacques. Once she has completed her scheme and revealed it to Jean, her role is played out – as the acceleration of Jean's car wipes her off the screen, for the last time, she has literally nothing more to do or say.

But if Maria Casarès's success is unanimously accepted, so is Paul Bernard's failure as Jean. As a specialist in portraying traitors and roués,

he might be considered obliquely not inappropriate – though Bresson wanted Alain Cuny or possibly Jean Marais. Evidently, the question is of sympathy, even identification. It is not so much that his screen presence and enunciation are inappropriate to the dramatic situation – which they are – as that it is difficult to participate in or care about his fate whether as victim of Hélène or as forgiving husband of Agnès; the weakness is particularly crucial at the end of the film. Lucienne Bogaert's strange, ambiguous portrayal of Mme D. seems to me exactly right. Elina Labourdette as Agnès is more open to question, but her odd falsities and occasionally irritating *gamine* quality are sometimes unexpectedly expressive – for instance, her brittle hardness and forced brightness at the rainy meeting with Jean in the Square de Pont-Royal. And, one real asset, of course, is her dancing, which is genuinely liberating, especially the second dance, in provincial costume.

Just as *Les Dames* was Bresson's last professionally acted film, so it was his last made primarily in the studio – anyway, it is mainly an indoor, enclosed, interior film; even outdoors, people are frequently inside cars or move into sheltering doorways. The photographic style is therefore different from the quasi-documentary realism of the Burel-shot films. Agostini, of a younger generation than his successor, apparently modelled himself on the best American examples of the late 'thirties. For instance, the lighting is carefully calculated and frequently expressive, though it is usually given some naturalistic justification, e.g. passing cars' headlamps and street lights flickering on Hélène's face, the lift descending, doors opening and closing, or the blaze of a fire. Sunlight is carefully differentiated in texture and mood from rain-filtered light. Tracking shots are much more frequent than in most Bresson films – he later relied more on precise and, if necessary, stylised framing, sometimes positively emphasising the camera's stillness against the movement in or into a frame. In *Les Dames*, the camera's movement is occasionally consciously emphasised, as in the long tracking shot which leads into Agnès's second meeting with Jean in the Bois, or the more subtle one where the camera sidles after Hélène into Mme D's flat in the earring episode. This flowing visual style is further enhanced by the high proportion of slow dissolves, rather than the fades-to-black which usually control the rhythm of Bresson's subsequent films. Sometimes the dissolves are ellipses or simply cover slight lapses of time or changes of place; but they can also make comments – for example, the recurrence of dissolves from medium shots of Mme D. to close-ups of Hélène, or vice versa, suggests a greater complicity between them than is ever spelled out.

The sound track is already distinctively Bressonian in its allusiveness, richness and ellipses, though the rather full and formal dialogue, along with a surplus of mood-setting music partially conceals the characteristic quality. A notable instance is Mme D's initial account of her plight to Hélène, punctuated by a slamming door, rattling, murmurs, louder rattling, Agnès's shout and the men's rowdy, half-drunken laughter. Another is the sound of the fountain in the Square de Pont-Royal, puzzlingly heard before it is seen, and reminiscent of the Cascade, scene of Jean's previous meeting with Agnès. Generally, the traffic noise of the Square and even of the Bois contrasts with the expensive hush of Hélène's neighbourhood. Final example: the inexorable steel shutters coming down to end Agnès's only day at work – one shutter seen, the other implied by sound and diminution of light; the technique parallels and anticipates the two cars sliding on oil in *Balthazar*.

A treatment of Bresson's style which covers only persons, camera effects and sounds clearly omits one of the most central elements, the expressive use of physical objects – for instance, the contrast at the wedding between Hélène's black dress and Agnès's white, as basic as in any cowboy movie, except that Agnès is looking and feeling increasingly guilty, while Hélène is unassailably (though pitiably) self-righteous. More characteristic, though less immediately striking, is the use of documents, including letters and photographs. Apart from the presumably social letters that are always awaiting Hélène as she returns from shopping – and which form, indeed, an apparently considerable element of her otherwise meagre social interchange – there are three important letters in the film: Agnès's to Hélène (dictated by Hélène), Jean's to Agnès, and Agnès's to Jean. The first alone is actually read, by Jean; only one sentence, but a key one, of the second is read: '*Je vous attendrai . . . tous les jours à la cascade.*' Agnès's true confession remains undelivered and is ultimately crumpled despairingly in her hand – a beautifully melancholy shot through the rain from outside her window. Similarly, the publicity photographs of Agnès in her dance costume, which would reveal the truth to Jean, are hidden by Mme D. so hastily that she knocks down the costume itself; but it is explicable as fancy dress, and so compatible with the earlier photographs of Agnès before her downfall.

The strong symbolic stress on animals in the late films has only one precursor here, Hélène's little white dog, which she always caresses and treats tenderly, if dominantly, even when, perhaps especially when, she is angry or hurt. Jean also sometimes fondles or takes care of it, but so absent-mindedly and indifferently that it invariably runs to her by choice – the extended panning shot late in the film following it from him to her even prompts the suspicion that it has somehow come to represent the love between them, so cherished by her and neglected by him.

More obviously, flowers have throughout the film an amorous significance, conventional in origin but subtly modified by changing con-texts – the dressing room, where Agnès angrily throws them on the floor; the florist's shop and Agnès's living room, Agnès being suspicious of Jean's gift but not actually rejecting; Hélène's in the lift, the day she has fixed for the first encounter in the Bois, these flowers being also presumably a gift from Jean but purely a conventional gesture now and without their former significance of courtship; the artificial flowers on the provincial dance

Still: *Elina Labourdette as Agnès. The photo-graph from her past which is seen in Jacques Demy's* Lola *(where she plays the young girl's mother) shows her in this costume.*

are never punished, at least apparently – even Michel's imprisonment for pickpocketing becomes a blessing in disguise. All Bresson's films have happy endings, at least by intention, and in terms of the success of projects – actually even the evil projects more often than not succeed. But the 'happy' ending usually consists of death or a symbolic death endured and transcended, in *Condamné* and perhaps *Pickpocket* as well as *Les Dames*. Such endings are happy in representing the triumph of love or trust or both – though qualified by a new bitterness in the late films.

But in *Les Dames* the finale is less persuasive than, say, the cryptic conclusion of *Pickpocket*, for several causes: Paul Bernard's theatrical rendition of Jean's lines, Agnès's reversion to the formal rhetoric of Mme des Arcis (particularly miscalculated in a near-deathbed scene), Agostini's over-elaborate concluding craneshot, Grünenwald's music, too explicitly emotional here. These deficiencies do not diminish Bresson's responsibility; the overall effect of the last sequence unexpectedly Hollywoodian in a pejorative sense, cannot be interpreted away and is surely at odds with the rest of the film. To see the film as essentially the tragedy of Hélène rather than the triumph of Jean and Agnès, as most French critics have done, is to negate the value of all Bresson's additions to his source and indeed to revert precisely to Diderot's own explicit comment on the narrated events. It has sometimes been suggested that an improved ending would be the suicide of Hélène – but this seems to me quite un-Bressonian. Perhaps a more effective and more justified change would have been a fourth and fatal heart-attack for Agnès, leaving Jean to mourn her at the moment when he discovers fully her love and his forgiveness.

costume, with the suggestion of freshness and unsophistication; Agnès's wedding flowers and the many others in the room where she has her heart attacks, so that they seem about to take on sinister funerary associations.

Similar observations might be made about other groups of objects, from cars to broken vessels, from tables to tears, from gifts to telephones. But it will be more useful to move on to larger patterns. As Susan Sontag points out, most of Bresson's films are structured by a task or project – in fact, usually by several which may be parallel (in *Condamné*) but more often are opposed (e.g. the Curé, the Comtesse and Chantal in *Journal*). *Les Dames* is a curious in-between case insofar as Hélène's desire for revenge, Jean's desire for Agnès and Agnès's aim of a decent, happy respectability, though apparently opposed, all lead to the same conclusion. Here, as in the other films, good projects may lead to salvation; but evil projects

Stills: Left– Agnès (Elina Labourdette). Right– Hélène (Maria Casarès).

40

LE JOURNAL D'UN CURE DE CAMPAGNE

RAYMOND DURGNAT

The young priest of Ambricourt is disheartened by the spiritual sullenness of his first parish, typified by old Fabregars who quibbles over the costs of his wife's funeral. The priest suffers from severe stomach pains which have reduced him to a diet of stale bread and wine, and is very conscious of his timidity and gaucheness, despite the caustic encouragement of his older and more robust colleague, the priest of Torcy. When the deputy Mayor calls to discuss the installation of electricity, the young priest is unable to speak to him about the goings-on at his weekly dances and spends a night sleepless with remorse and guilt. His high hopes in one of the girls in his communion class, Seraphita Dumonchel, are disappointed when, while her comrades titter behind the door, she tells him that if she learns her lessons well it is not because of her piety but for the sake of the priest's beautiful eyes.

Gradually he is drawn into the situation at the castle of the local Count, from whom he hopes to get support for a projected youth club. The count's young daughter, Chantal, seethes with hatred of life because her governess, Mlle Louise, is her father's mistress; while the Countess, embittered by the death of her baby son many years ago feels love for no living creature.

The priest consults a rough country doctor, Dr Delbende, a gruff but noble agnostic, who diagnoses inherited alcoholism. The priest is besieged by despair night after night; receives anonymous letters, and is shocked by the presumed suicide of Dr Delbende. Fearing that a crisis is imminent at the castle, he tries to consult the Curé of Torcy. But the latter is absent and the young man has to face his tests alone. After a visit from Chantal, who is also contemplating suicide, the priest manages to restore the Countess's faith; she dies during the night. Chantal browbeats her father into abruptly dismissing the governess, and spitefully accuses the priest of having been responsible for her mother's death. The Count takes the complaint to high quarters; the Curé refuses to produce in his own defence a last letter from the Countess, and his superior, a sly and worldly Canon, respects the young priest's respect for the Countess's letter.

On his parish rounds, the priest faints and falls into a patch of mud; he is found and cared for by Seraphita. Chantal visits him again; she seems free from the temptation to commit suicide, but is still determined to go, if necessary, to the limits of evil. She is impressed despite herself when the priest offers to answer for her, 'soul for soul'.

On his way to consult a doctor in Lille, the priest meets Chantal's brother Olivier, a foreign legionnaire who offers him a lift on his motor-bike; the priest enjoys the exhilaration of the ride, but feels that, if he has been allowed to taste the pleasures of youth, it is only to make his sacrifice more complete. The doctor diagnoses advanced stomach cancer.

The young priest goes to a café to recover, and the proprietress's well-meant remarks pour

Still: the country priest (Claude Laydu).

42

salt on his wounds. He decides to visit Dufréty, an old friend of his seminary days, and finds him living in sin without health, faith or prospects. Dufréty assures his visitor that his tired, uneducated mistress 'counted for nothing in my intellectual evolution'. The priest falls ill and is cared for by Dufréty's mistress, who has totally sacrificed herself for her lover's sake, even refusing to marry him in case he should one day wish to return to his vocation. As he lies dying, the young priest is able to persuade him to call on the priest of Torcy; his last words are 'All is grace!'

Already before Bresson, Jean Aurenche and Pierre Bost, the celebrated pushmi-pullyu of French scriptwriting, had prepared an adaptation which for one reason or another failed to meet with the novelist's approval. Bresson discussed the subject with Bernanos before the latter's death, and aimed throughout at a maximum fidelity to the novel. Whereas Aurenche and Bost are specialists at inventing new episodes which correspond, often very closely, to the spirit of the original material, Bresson treated the novel as his 'reality', which he re-edited, concentrated, simplified, but to which he added nothing. Every phrase in the film is taken from the novel – although often shifted from one context to another. Aurenche and Bost's approach is 'additive', Bresson's 'subtractive'.

The final script was approved by Bernanos's literary executor and the film produced by UGC (the nationalised sector of the French film industry). Before shooting, Bresson, after ruling out all non-believers, interviewed over 100 candidates for the main part and finally chose Laydu, whom he met through Becker. At 24, Laydu, a Belgian-born Swiss, had never made a film, but had acted on the stage with

Still: the priest and the Count's daughter, Chantal (Nicole Ladmiral).

Barrault. Bresson met him every Sunday for a year, to talk to him about the role, to talk him *into* the role. This effort of persuasion, almost brainwashing, is an interesting counterpoint to Bresson's reputation for treating his actors like toys, of requiring them to speak their lines in a monotone and with as little expression as possible. His aim seems to be to attain a conviction without self-awareness (thus Laydu only realised that he had been portraying a saint when he saw the completed film). Bresson's way of frustrating the actor recalls the director par excellence of empty self-awareness – Antonioni.

In any event, Ladyu's performance represents a consummate effort at total identification with his role. He lived for many weeks with a group of young priests, absorbing their mannerisms and gestures, and during shooting starved himself so as to acquire the authentic mask of illness. Even his clothes are 'authentic' – the cassock was lent by one priest, the boots by another.

Like Dreyer, Bresson casts for character rather than 'acting ability' (after *Un Condamné à mort s'est echappé* he vowed he would never use professional actors again). The Curé de Torcy is played by Bresson's doctor, and there is a sad irony in the casting of Nicole Ladmiral (which often seems to happen when one casts for 'authenticity'). Chantal half-threatens to commit suicide and the Countess pooh-poohs the idea. A few years later, Nicole Ladmiral commited suicide.

The film was shot on location, in the countryside which Bernanos described as the village of Equilles in the Pas-de-Calais, a few miles from Ambricourt, which had been heavily devastated by the war. The cast 'camped out' on location during shooting, which lasted three months, longer than expected owing to unsuitably fine weather. After shooting, Bresson cut 45 minutes of the film's 160. All the omitted scenes concentrate on the priest's relationships with the parish rather than on the priest himself. In the English version, the 'commentary' – or rather the voice of the 'diary' – is dubbed by a voice with a faintly BBC-Anglican tinge, but the effect is soon neutralised by the film's intensity and by the quiet sensitivity of the English voice.

Despite Bresson's vow of fidelity, the film has an important shift of emphasis which may be symbolised in the person of the Curé de Torcy. Jean Sémolué suggests that the young priest's diary is Bernanos's record of his own inner struggles; but if the Curé of Ambricourt is Bernanos's inner self, the Curé de Torcy, with his long, angry, generous tirades on every topic under the sun is Bernanos's outer self. In fact in the novel the diary is less of a monologue than a dialogue. The relationship of the two priests has another sense; the Curé de Torcy representing the nagging but devoted voice of common sense, the church which continues in the world, while the Curé of Ambricourt is the church of purity, of sacrifice. In Bresson's film, however, Torcy seems cowed by the film's mood; his voice is more subdued, his eyes downcast, his gestures more restrained than one would imagine from the choleric rhythms of his harangues in the novel. He becomes little more than an 'outsider'. In one way Bresson's preoccupation with his hero is an improvement over Bernanos's besetting temptation, to attack agnostic materialism in the crudest terms.

In the novel, the diary is 'transparent', a convention, the priest would a) have had to have been born a novelist and b) spent most of the day writing up his diary. Bresson shows us the diary, an exercise book in which the Curé scribbles a few trite words before a flashback takes over. The shots of the diary's pages, far from being unfilmic are the cornerstone of the film's mood – the dull pages, their schoolroom atmosphere are visual symbols for the priest's childlike, obedient mind.

It is easy to see why Bresson has rejected conventional 'realism' – which, in effect, means that the director has to record many inessential and superficial feelings, whims and fluctuations in his characters' experiences. But a man's soul is more sullen, mysterious, withdrawn. In Bresson the monotone and the dead-pan represent, not a mask, but a revelation of the essential man. His personages seem aloof because they are naked. There is no question of expressionism rather than realism. The physical is spiritualised; the eternal verities permeate the material world. The location photography – 'neo-realism' – express not just a particular place, a 'mood', but a spiritual condition of man without God. The landscapes have a sad dejection reminiscent of many Franju films – another occult coincidence, for the commentary of Le Sang des Bêtes is spoken, in a deliberate monotone, by – Nicole Ladmiral.

The union of spiritual and material is suggested by another partial affinity, that of Bresson and Dreyer. Dreyer is more physical, more concerned with flesh, he photographs like a sculptor; whereas Bresson, more suave, veiled and fine, works as much through atmospheres, through a semi-reticence. Of all Dreyer's films, his last, Ordet, is the nearest to Bresson's. But both directors 'brainwash' their actors, and feel through faces; Henri Agel remarks how the nervous sincerity of the young priest is 'exposed in the round, almost doll-like face of Claude Laydu, whose pain-filled eyes alone give an air of maturity to the as yet hardly formed human clay. But, for all this his countenance has the strength needed for loving, for suffering, for enduring blows! As malleable as the softest clay, the soul which is revealed through this face can offer no resistance to the terrible love of God which will make it bleed copiously...'

The opening shot of the Count and his mistress embracing behind the grille, and abruptly separating as the priest catches sight of them, make any more elaborate explanation unnecessary; everything is there, in their faces, their movements, the atmosphere a dank shame, a dry joylessness like death, the Count's strange mixture of cowardice and coldness. This intense 'physicality' and 'materialism' explain how the film feels so intense even though, dramatically, there is so little emphasis and so many omissions.

The mechanics of the plot are described, simply, by the commentary; we see only the essential moment of each scene, a moment which acquires an eerie concentration from this isolation and emphasis. Often, paradoxically, the essential moment of each scene is omitted. For example, the 'voice of the diary' tells us that the priest 'makes the gesture of total acceptance', which is presumably stretching himself out on the floor of his bedroom in the posture of the cross; but all we see is the priest hauling himself up by the bedrail, afterwards. And this extraordinary omission provides the clue to Bresson's whole method. What matters is not the gesture itself – which might appeal to the spectator for the wrong reasons (its apparent rhetoric), but the fact of the gesture – the

Still: the priests of Ambricourt and of Torcy.

attempted contact with God, the attempted self-discipline, and the fact that the gesture does *not* bring relief. And it is all in his face . . .

The film's ellipses culminate in the final shot, where the seen world fades away altogether, to be replaced by a one-and-a-half-minute shot of a plain cross, while the voice of the Curé de Torcy concludes the account of his friend's death. Of this climax (which incidentally is adumbrated in Dreyer's *Day of Wrath*), André Bazin wrote, 'At the point which Bresson has reached, the image can become more eloquent only by disappearing altogether' – a paradox which at first seems a negation of cinema, especially if one's ideal of cinema is an everlasting chase. Yet Bazin is quite right, for the final shot of the cross acquires its meaning by its relationship to the drama, by the way in which it 'supplants' the physical world, that is, by the venerable cinematic principle of montage. Bresson's film is firmly rooted in the *physical* – in the reflection of cancer in the priest's face – and the cross is an image of its total sacrifice. The spiritual has devoured the flesh. Bazin, perhaps a shade too schematically, describes the film as a dialectic of 'commentary versus image', which seems to me to be only one form of the deeper dialectic, between the lyrical tension and the dramatic ellipse – which implies a 'superdramatic', that is, a supernatural source of feeling (the soul, God). As Bazin says, 'The film's most moving moments are those where the commentary repeats exactly what the image is showing' – another mortal sin according to the dogmas of filmcraft. But the effect is moving because, by being there, the commentary goes further than the image. The priest's words have the extra precision, the sharpness, the gratuitousness, which corresponds to a childlike – or Godlike – intuition. He has 'realised', because of his tormenting hypersensitivity, something we vaguely sensed, wondered about, but could not quite *see*. The episode where he *guesses* that Chantal has a letter, and that letter is a suicide letter, is an outstanding example; but the effect is present in many subtler ways. At other times, the priest imagines a feeling which isn't there. For example, he feels that the Count is a 'friend', whereas we remain sceptical, the Count's face is too cold, we ask ourselves how the priest could possibly think he is a friend, we sense that the priest is imagining the friend he so badly longs for. The matter-of-fact material world is evoked above all in the sounds; the sullen scrabble of the rake on the path during the priest's battle for the Countess's soul, the sound of automobiles swishing past the signpost 'Ambricourt' which establishes the setting of the spiritual tragedy as an obscure hamlet of no importance. The constant use of 'voices off' reduces conversations to discarnate contacts, between souls and eternal truth, rather than between the superficial politenesses of people.

It is certainly fair to say that the priest's lack of joy is the result, not of sheer goodness, but of a deep-rooted guilt complex. But I can't agree with those critics who seem to assume that if a film's hero is foolish, immature, weak or unsympathetic, this is in some way a point against the film. On the contrary. Saints don't have to be perfect and this film would not only be ludicrous, but quite impossible, if its hero were a pious pantechnicon of all possible virtues. Of course the priest 'morbidly' makes himself more miserable than he 'should' – the episode with Seraphita during his communion class is an example. Yet perhaps his humourlessness here is a response to Seraphita's real feelings – whereas humour would be simply a cowardly way of restoring his own ease of soul. The kernel of the film is: 'How wonderful that we can give others that peace which we ourselves do not possess. Oh miracle of our empty hands.'

An additional source of obscurity is that

Still: the priest and the countess.

several scenes hinge on issues unfamiliar to non-Christians. Thus the 'duel' (too hostile a word, perhaps) between the Countess and the Curé depends on her defiant cry, 'I would rather be with my son in Hell than separated from him in Heaven.' The priest's anguish enables her to see that her indignation against God on behalf of her son conceals a possessiveness which would not shrink from his destruction (bringing him to Hell). Later she throws his photograph in the fire, and the priest retrieves it for her – such renunciation is also excessive.

A persistent, but insistent, ellipse is the question of despair and suicide. The word is several times led up to, but never quite uttered. Indeed the dialectic of suicide and sacrifice is one of the 'concealed themes' of the novel, and several times their near-identity is hinted at. The Countess dies immediately after finding peace of soul, and there is a hint that her death was somehow 'provoked' by her conversion: she is now 'free' from sin, free to die. The young Curé, a hereditary alcoholic (Original Sin?) has nourished himself on bread and wine (the Sacraments?). Yet the symbol of sin and salvation, wine, is the same. And the priest's alcoholism has concealed a cancer – which is, so to speak, a rebellion 'of' the body against the spirit – something malignant and suicidal, foreign to the priest yet within him, like the devil.

Whereas Protestant writers are comparatively untroubled by questions of strict orthodoxy, few important Roman Catholic artists have escaped charges of heresy from their co-religionaries. Graham Greene, Mauriac and Bernanos himself have been favourite targets, and these days the accusation is almost always of Manicheanism or of Jansenism (two words enjoying a mild vogue in highbrow circles, even non-Christian ones; one never hears of literary critics censuring a novelist for, say, his Pelagianism). The severity and austerity of Bresson's emotional range and style undoubtedly justify the common comparison with two celebrated Jansenists, Racine and Pascal; and there is a quiet stress on the importance of integrity and strength of will which brings Bresson nearer nonconformism even than Jansenism.

Le Journal d'un curé de campagne seems to me thoroughly orthodox in asserting *simultaneously* the strength of the submitting will and the inexorability of divine grace. Possibly the range of experience with which Bresson deals would be incomplete, and in that sense heretical, if advanced as a total or normative description of Christianity. But if one asks oneself whether the range of experience within which Bresson is 'at home' lies within the possibilities of Roman Catholic (or for that matter Protestant) orthodoxy surely we have to answer that it does. It seems quite possible that God would allow a parish priest to endure so much suffering with so little joy; or what's a heaven for?

Bresson's film is that rare phenomenon, a Christian tragedy, rare precisely because tragedy implies that in this life at least good is pulverised while the evil flourish as the green bay tree; too many Christian moralists seem strangely anxious to assert that good and evil will earn their due reward here and now even if by some mischance there is no life after death. Yet it is because the saint stakes everything on his faith that Christianity has its tragic heroism (and not just the cringing prudence of Pascal's notorious bet). It is essential to the film, as to the novel, that the priest's suffering be maximal, his 'joy' obliterated, and that he reach the limit of experience. Professor Bosanquet once remarked that 'only that optimism is worth its salt which can go all the way with pessimism and arrive at a point beyond it'; in Bresson's film the final exaltation is derived neither by mitigating nor by complacently embracing suffering, and, here, it seems to me, lies its greatness and humanity.

LE JOURNAL D'UN CURE DE CAMPAGNE

ANDRE BAZIN

If *The Diary of a Country Priest* impresses us as a masterpiece, and this with an almost physical impact, if it moves the critic and the uncritical alike, it is primarily because of its power to stir the emotions, rather than the intelligence, at their highest level of sensitivity. The temporary eclipse of *Les Dames du Bois de Boulogne* was for precisely the opposite reason. This film could not stir us unless we had, if not exactly analysed, at least tested its intellectual structure and, so to speak, understood the rules of the game.

While the instantaneous success of *Le Journal* is undeniable, the aesthetic principles on which it is based are nevertheless the most paradoxical, maybe even the most complex, ever manifest in a sound film. Hence the refrain of those critics, ill-equipped to understand it. 'Paradoxical,' they say, 'incredible – an unprecedented success that can never be repeated.' Thus they renounce any attempt at explanation and take refuge in the perfect alibi of a stroke of genius. On the other hand, among those whose aesthetic preferences are of a kind with Bresson's and whom one would have unhesitatingly thought to be his allies, there is a deep sense of disappointment in proportion as they expected greater acts of daring from him.

First embarrassed, then irritated by the realisation of what the director did not do, yet too long in accord with him to be able to change their views on the spot; too caught up in his style to recapture their intellectual virginity which would have left the way open to emotion, they have neither understood nor liked the film.

Thus we find the critical field divided into two extreme groups. At one end those least equipped to understand *Le Journal* and who, by the same token, have loved it all the more without knowing why; at the other end those 'happy few' who, expecting something different, have not liked it and have failed to understand it. It is the strangers to the cinema, the men of letters, amazed that they could so love a film and be capable of freeing their minds of prejudice, who have understood what Bresson had in mind more clearly than anyone else.

Admittedly Bresson has done his best to cover his tracks. His avowal of fidelity to the original from the first moment that he embarked on the adaptation, his declared intention of following the book word-for-word conditioned us to look for just that and the film only serves to prove it. Unlike Aurenche and Bost, who were preoccupied with the optics of the screen and the balance of their drama in its new form, Bresson, instead of building up the minor characters like the parents in *Le Diable au corps*, eliminated them. He prunes even the very essentials, giving an impression as he does so of a fidelity unable to sacrifice one single word without a pucker of concern and a thousand preliminary twinges of remorse. Again this pruning is always in the interest of simplification, never of addition. It is no exaggeration to say that if Bernanos had written the screenplay he would have taken greater liberties with his novel. He had, indeed, explicitly recognised the right of the adaptor to make use of his book according to the requirements of the cinema, the right that is 'to dream his story over'.

However, if we praise Bresson for his fidelity, it is for the most insidious kind of fidelity, a most pervasive form of creative licence. Of course, one clearly cannot adapt without transposing. In that respect, Bernanos was on the side of aesthetic common sense. Literal translations are not the faithful ones. The changes that Aurenche and Bost made to *Le Diable au corps* are almost all entirely justified in principle. A character on the screen and the same character as evoked by the novelist are not identical.

Valéry condemned the novel for being obliged to record that 'the Marquise had tea at five o'clock'. On his side, the novelist might in turn pity the film-maker for having to show the marquise actually at the table. It is for this reason that the relatives of the heroes in Radiguet, peripheral in the novel, appear important on the screen. The adaptor, however, must be as concerned with the text as with the characters and with the threat of their physical presence to the balance of the story. Having transformed the narrative into visuals, the film-maker must put the rest into dialogue, including the existing dialogue of the novel although we expect some modification of the latter – since spoken as written, its effectiveness and even its meaning will normally evaporate.

It is here that we see the paradoxical effect of the textual fidelity of *Le Journal*.

While the characters in the book are presented to the reader in high relief and while their inevitably brief evocation by the pen of the curé of Ambricourt never gives us a feeling of frustration or of any limits being put both to their existence and to our knowledge of their existence, Bresson, in the process of showing them to us, is forever hurrying them out of sight. In place of the powerfully concrete evocations of the novelist, the film offers us an increasingly impoverished image which escapes us because it is hidden from us and is never really developed.

The novel of Bernanos is rich in picturesque evocations, solid, concrete, strikingly visual. For example: 'The Count went out – his excuse the rain. With every step the water oozed from his long boots. The three or four rabbits he had shot were lumped together in the bottom of his game-bag in a horrible-looking little pile of bloodstained mud and grey hair. He had hung the string bag on the wall and as he talked to me I saw fixed on me, through the intertwining cords, a still limpid and gentle eye.'

Do you feel you have seen all this somewhere before? Don't bother to look where. It was probably in a Renoir film. Now compare this scene with the other in which the Count brings the two rabbits to the presbytery – admittedly this comes later in the book but the two could have profitably been combined, thus giving them a style in common – and if you still have any doubts, Bresson's own admission will remove them. Forced to throw out a third of his final cut for the exhibitor's copy he ended, as we know, by declaring with a delicate touch of cynicism that he was delighted to have had to do so. Actually, the only 'visual' he really cared about was the blank screen at the finale, which we will discuss later.

If he had really been faithful to the book, Bresson would have made quite a different film. Determined though he was to add nothing to the original – already a subtle form of betrayal by omission – he might at least have chosen to sacrifice the more literary parts for the many passages of ready-made film material that cried out for visualisation. Yet he systematically took the opposite course. When you compare the two, it is the film that is literary while the novel teems with visual material.

The way he handles the text is even more revealing. He refuses to put into dialogue (I hardly dare to say 'film dialogue') those passages from the novel where the curé enters in his

Still: the Count and the priest.

diary the report of such-and-such a conversation. Here is a first discrepancy, since Bernanos at no point guarantees that the curé is giving a word-for-word report of what he heard. The odds are that he is not. In any event, supposing he *is*, and that Bresson has it in mind to preserve, along with the objective image, the subjective character of something remembered, it is still true that the mental and emotional impact of a line that is merely read is very different from that of a spoken line.

Now, not only does he not adapt the dialogue, however circumspectly, to the demands of a performance, he goes out of his way, on the contrary, whenever the text of the novel has the rhythm and balance of true dialogue, to prevent the actor from bringing out these qualities. Thus a good deal of excellent dramatic dialogue is thrown away because of the flat monotone in which the director insists that it be delivered.

Many complimentary things have been said about *Les Dames du Bois de Boulogne*, very little about the adaptation. The critics have, to all intents and purposes, treated the film as if it was made from an original screenplay. The outstanding quality of the dialogue has been attributed to Cocteau, whose reputation has little need of such praise. This is because they have not re-read *Jacques le fataliste*, in which they would have found if not the entire script, at least the evidence of a subtle game of hide and go seek, word for word, with the text of Diderot. While it did not make one feel one ought to go back to verify the fact at close quarters, the modern version left one with the impression that Bresson had taken liberties with the story and retained simply the situation and, if you like, a certain eighteenth-century flavour. Since, in addition, he had killed off two or three writers under him, so to speak, it was reasonable to suppose that he was that many steps away from the original. However I recommend fans of the *Dames du Bois de Boulogne* and aspiring scenarists alike to take a second look at the film with these considerations in mind. Without intending in any way to detract from the decisive part played by the style of the direction in the success of the film, it is important to examine very closely the foundations of this success, namely a marvellously subtle interplay – a sort of counterpart between faithfulness and unfaithfulness to the original.

It has been suggested in criticism of *Les Dames du Bois de Boulogne*, with equal proportions of good sense and misunderstanding, that the psychological make-up of the characters is out of key with the society in which they are shown as living. True, it is the mores of the time that, in the novel of Diderot, justify the choice of the revenge and give it its effectiveness. It is true again that this same revenge seems to the modern spectator to be something out of the blue, something beyond his experience. It is equally useless on the other hand for those who defend the film to look for any sort of social justification for the characters. Prostitution and pandering as shown in the novel are facts with a very clear and solid contemporary social context. In the film of *Les Dames* they are all the more mystifying since they have no basic justification. The revenge of an injured mistress who forces her unfaithful lover to marry a luscious cabaret dancer seems to us to be a ridiculous gesture. Nor can the fact that the characters appear to be abstractions be explained by deliberate cuts made by the director during the filming. They are that way in the script. The reason Bresson does not tell us more about his characters is not because he has no desire to, but because he would be hard put to do so. Racine does not describe the colour of the wallpaper in the rooms to which his characters retire. To this one may answer, of course, that classical tragedy has no need of the alibis of realism and that this is one of the basic differences between the theatre and the cinema. That is true enough. It is also precisely why Bresson does not derive his cinematographic abstraction simply from the bare episodes but from the counterpoint that the reality of the situation sets up with itself. In *Les Dames du Bois de Boulogne*, Bresson has taken the risk of transferring one realistic story into the context of another. The result is that these two examples of realism cancel one another out, the passions displayed emerge out of the characters as if from a chrysalis, the action from the twists and turns of the plot, and the tragedy from the trappings of the drama. The sound of a windshield-wiper against a page of Diderot is all it took to turn it into Racinian dialogue. Obviously Bresson is not aiming at absolute realism. On the other hand, his stylised treatment of it does not have the pure abstract quality of a symbol. It is rather a structured presentation of the abstract and concrete, that is to say of the reciprocal interplay of seemingly incompatible elements. The rain, the murmur of a waterfall, the sound of earth pouring from a broken pot, the hooves of a horse on the cobblestones, are not there just as a contrast to the simplification of the sets or the convention of the costumes, still less as a contrast to the literary and anachronistic flavour of the dialogue. They are not needed either for dramatic antithesis or for a contrast in decor. They are there deliberately as neutrals, as foreign bodies, like a grain of sand that gets into and seizes up a piece of machinery. If the arbitrariness of their choice resembles an abstraction, it is the abstraction of the concrete integral. They are like lines drawn across an image to affirm its transparency, as the dust affirms the transparency of a diamond; it is impurity at its purest.

This interaction of sound and decor is repeated in the very midst of elements which seem at first to be completely stylised. For example, the two apartments of the women are almost totally unfurnished, but this calculated bareness has its explanation. That the frames should be on the walls though the paintings have been sold is undoubtedly a deliberate touch of realism. The abstract whiteness of the new apartment is not intended as part of a pattern of theatrical expressionism. The apartment is white because it has just been repainted and the smell of fresh paint still hangs about. Is there any need to add to this list the elevator or the concierge's telephone, or, on the soundtrack, the tumult of male voices that follows the face-slapping of Agnès, the text for which reads totally conventionally while the sound quality of it is absolute perfection.

I have referred to *Les Dames* in discussing *Le Journal* because it is important to point out the profound similarity between the mechanics of their respective adaptations.

The style of *Le Journal* indicates a more systematic searching, a rigour that is almost unbearable. It was made under very different technical conditions. Yet we shall see that the procedure was in each case basically the same. In both it was a matter of getting to the heart of a story or of a drama, of achieving the most rigorous form of aesthetic abstraction while avoiding expressionism by way of an interplay of literature and realism, which added to its cinematic potential while seeming to negate it. In any case, Bresson's faithfulness to his model is the alibi of liberty in chains. If he is faithful to the text this is because it serves his purpose better than taking useless liberties. Furthermore, this respect for the letter is, in the last analysis, far more than an exquisite embarrassment, it is a dialectical moment in the creation of a style.

So it is pointless to complain that paradoxically Bresson is at one and the same time the slave and the master of his text, because it is precisely from this seeming contradiction that he gets his effects. Henri Agel, for example, describes the film as a page of Victor Hugo rewritten in the style of de Nerval. But surely one could imagine poetic results born of this monstrous coupling, of unexpectedly revealing flashes touched off by a translation made not just from one language into another (like Mallarmé's translation of Poe) but from one style and one content into the style of another artist and from the material of one art transposed into the material of another.

Let us look a little more closely now at *Le Journal* and see what in it has not really come off. While not wishing to praise Bresson for all his weak spots, for there are weaknesses, rare ones, which work to his disadvantage, we can say quite definitely that they are all an integral part of his style; they are simply that kind of awkwardness to which a high degree of sensibility may lead, and if Bresson has any reason here for self-congratulation, it is for having had the sense to see in that awkwardness the price he must pay for something more important.

So, even if the acting in general seems poor,

except for Laydu all the time and for Nicole Ladmiral some of it, this, provided you like the film, will only appear to be a minor defect. But now we have to explain why Bresson who directed his cast so superbly in *Les Anges du péché* and *Les Dames du Bois de Boulogne* seems to handle them in this film as amateurishly as any tyro with a camera who has roped in his aunt and the family lawyer. Do people really imagine that it was easier to get Maria Casarès to play down her talent than to handle a group of docile amateurs ? Certainly some scenes were poorly acted. It is odd however that these were by no means the least moving.

The fact is that this film is not to be measured by ordinary standards of acting. It is important to remember that the · cast were all either amateurs or simple beginners. *Le Journal* no more approximates to *Bicycle Thieves* than to *L'Entrée des artistes*. Actually the only film it can be likened to is Carl Dreyer's *Jeanne d'Arc*. The cast is not being asked to act out a text, not even to live it out, just to speak it. It is because of this that the passages spoken off-screen so perfectly match the passages spoken by the characters on-screen. There is no fundamental difference either in tone or style. This plan of attack not only rules out any dramatic interpretation by the actors but also any psychological touches either. What we are asked to look for on their faces is not some fleeting reflection of the words but an uninterrupted condition of soul, the outward revelation of an interior destiny.

Thus this so-called badly acted film leaves us with the feeling of having seen a gallery of portraits whose expressions could not be other than they were. In this respect the most characteristic of all is of Chantal in the confessional. Dressed in black, withdrawn into the shadows, Nicole Ladmiral allows us only a glimpse of a

Still: the priest and his parish.

56

mask, half lit, half in shadow, like a seal stamped on wax, all blurred at the edges.

Naturally Bresson, like Dreyer, is only concerned with the countenance as flesh, which, when not involved in playing a role, is a man's true imprint, the most visible mark of his soul. It is then that the countenance takes on the dignity of a sign. He would have us be concerned here not with the psychology but with the physiology of existence. Hence the hieratic tempo of the acting, the slow ambiguous gestures, the obstinate recurrence of certain behavioural patterns, the unforgettable dreamlike slow motion. Nothing purely accidental could happen to these people – confirmed as each is in his own way of life, essentially concerned either against the influence of grace, to continue so, or, responding to grace, to throw off the deadly Nessus-mantle of the old Adam.

There is no development of character. Their inner conflicts, the various phases of their struggle as they wrestle with the Angel of the Lord, are never outwardly revealed. What we see is rather a concentration of suffering, the recurrent spasms of childbirth or of a snake sloughing off its skin. We can truly say that Bresson strips his characters bare.

Eschewing psychological analysis, the film in consequence lies outside the usual dramatic categories. The succession of events is not constructed according to the usual laws of dramaturgy under which the passions work towards a soul-satisfying climax. Events do indeed follow one another according to a necessary order, yet within a framework of accidental happenings. Free acts and coincidences are interwoven. Each moment in the film, each set-up, has its own due measure, alike, of freedom and of necessity. They all move in the same direction, but separately like iron filings drawn to the overall surface of a magnet. If the word tragedy comes to one's pen, it is in an opposite sense since we can only

be dealing here with a tragedy freely willed. The transcendence of the Bernanos–Bresson universe is not the transcendence of destiny as the ancients understood it, nor yet the transcendence of Racinian passion, but the transcendence of grace which is something each of us is free to refuse.

If, nevertheless, the concatenation of events and the causal efficiency of the characters involved appear to operate just as rigidly as in a traditional dramatic structure, it is because they are responding to an order, of prophecy (or perhaps one should say of Kirkegaardian 'repetition') that is as different from fatality as causality is from analogy.

The pattern of the film's unfolding is not that of tragedy in the usual sense, rather in the sense of the mediaeval Passion Play, or better still, of the Way of the Cross, each sequence being a station along that road. We are given the key to this by the dialogue in the hut between the two curés, when the one from Ambricourt reveals that he is spiritually attracted to the Mount of Olives. 'Is it not enough that Our Lord should have granted me the grace of letting me know today, through the words of my old teacher, that nothing, throughout all eternity, can remove me from the place chosen by me from all eternity, that I was the prisoner of His Sacred Passion?'

Death is not the preordained end of our final agony, only its conclusion and a deliverance. Henceforth we shall know to what divine ordinance, to what spiritual rhythm the sufferings and actions of the curé respond. They are the outward representation of his agony. At which point one should indicate the analogies with Christ that abound towards the end of the film, or they may very well go unnoticed. For example, the two fainting fits during the night; the fall in the mud; the vomitings of wine and blood – a remarkable synthesis of powerful comparisons with the falls of Jesus, the Blood of the Passion, the sponge with vinegar on it, and the defiling spittle. These are not all. For the veil of Veronica we have the cloth of Seraphita; then finally the death in the attic – a Golgotha with even a good and a bad thief.

Now let us immediately put aside these comparisons, the very enumeration of which is necessarily deceptive. Their aesthetic weight derives from their theological value, but both defy explanation. Bresson like Bernanos avoids any sort of symbolic allusion and so none of the situations, despite their obvious parallel to the Gospel, is created precisely because of that parallel. Each carries its own biographical and individual meaning. Its Christ-like resemblance comes second, through being projected on to the higher plane of analogy. In no sense is it true to say that the life of the curé of Ambricourt is an imitation of its divine model; rather it is a repetition and a picturing forth of that life. Each bears his own cross and each cross is different, but all are the Cross of the Passion. The sweat on the brow of the curé is a bloody sweat.

Still: Seraphita cares for the priest.

So, probably for the first time, the cinema gives us a film in which the only genuine incidents, the only perceptible movements are those of the life of the spirit. Not only that, it also offers us a new dramatic form that is specifically religious – or better still, specifically theological; a phenomenology of salvation and grace.

It is worth noting that through playing down the psychological elements and keeping the dramatics to a minimum, Bresson is left to face two kinds of pure reality. On the one hand, as we saw, we have the countenance of the actor denuded of all symbolic expression, sheer epidermis, set in a surrounding devoid of any artifice. On the other hand there is what we must call the 'written reality'. Indeed, Bresson's faithfulness to the text of Bernanos, his refusal, that is, not only to adapt it but also his paradoxical concern to emphasise its literary character, is part of the same predetermined approach to the direction of his actors and the selection of his settings. Bresson treats the novel as he does his characters. The novel is a cold, hard fact, a reality to be accepted as it stands. One must not attempt to adapt it to the situation in hand, or manipulate it to fit some passing need for an explanation; on the contrary it is something to be taken absolutely as it stands. Bresson never condenses the text, he cuts it. Thus what is left over is a part of the original. Like marble from a quarry the words of the film continue to be part of the novel. Of course the deliberate emphasis on their literary character can be interpreted as a search after artistic stylisation, which is the very opposite of realism. The fact is, however, that in this case the reality is not the descriptive content, moral or intellectual, of the text – it is the very text itself, or more properly, the style. Clearly the reality at one stage removed of the novel and that which the camera captures directly, cannot fit or grow together or become one. On the contrary the effect of their juxtaposition is to reaffirm their differences. Each plays its part, side by side, using the means at its disposal, in its own setting and after its own style. But it is doubtless by this separating off of elements which because of their resemblance would appear to belong together, that Bresson manages to eliminate what is accidental. The ontological conflict between two orders of events, occurring simultaneously, when confronted on the screen reveal their single common measure – the soul.

Each actor says the same things and the very disparity between their expressions, the substance of what they say, their style, the kind of indifference which seems to govern the relation of actor to text, of word and visage, is the surest guarantee of their close complicity. This language which no lips could speak is, of necessity, from the soul.

It is unlikely that there exists anywhere in the whole of French cinema, perhaps even in all French literature, many moments of a more intense beauty than in the medallion scene between the curé and the Countess. Its beauty does not derive from the acting nor from the psychological and dramatic values of the dialogue, nor indeed from its intrinsic meaning. The true dialogue that punctuates the struggle between the inspired priest and a soul in despair is, of its very nature, ineffable. The decisive clashes of their spiritual fencing-match escape us. Their words announce, or prepare the way for, the fiery touch of grace. There is nothing here then of the flow of words that usually goes with a conversion, while the overpowering severity of the dialogue, its rising tension and its final calm leave us with the conviction that we have been the privileged witnesses of a supernatural storm. The words themselves are so much dead weight, the echo of a silence that is the true dialogue between these two souls; a hint at their secret; the opposite side of the coin, if one dare say so, of the Divine Countenance. When later the curé refuses to come to his own defence by producing the Countess' letter, it is not out of humility or love of suffering. It is rather because no tangible evidence is worthy to play a part either in his defence or his indictment. Of its nature the evidence of the Countess is no more acceptable than that of Chantal, and none has the right to ask God to bear witness.

The technique of Bresson's direction cannot adequately be judged except at the level of his aesthetic intention. Inadequately as we may have so far described the latter, it may yet be that the highly astonishing paradox of the film is now a little more evident. Actually the distinction of having set text over against image

Still: Diary of a Country Priest.

for the first time goes to Melville in his *Silence de la mer*. It is noteworthy that his reason was likewise a desire for fidelity. However, the structure of Vercors's book was of itself unusual. In his *Journal* Bresson has done more than justify Melville's experiment and shown how well warranted it was. He has carried it to its final conclusions.

Is *Le Journal* just a silent film with spoken titles? The spoken word, as we have seen, does

Stills: Louise, the governess (Nicole Maurey) with the priest (above), and with Chantal and her father, who is Louise's lover (right).

not enter into the image as a realistic component. Even when spoken by one of the characters, it rather resembles the recitative of an opera. At first sight the film seems to be somehow made up on the one hand of the abbreviated text of the novel and illustrated, on

the other hand, by images that never pretend to replace it. All that is spoken is not seen, yet nothing is seen that is not also spoken. At worst, critical good sense can reproach Bresson with having substituted an illustrated radio-phonic montage, no less, for Bernanos's novel.

So it is from this ostensible corruption of the art of cinema that we begin if we are to grasp fully Bresson's originality and boldness.

In the first place, if Bresson 'returns' to the silent film it is certainly not, despite the abundance of close-ups, because he wants to tie in again with theatrical expressionism – that fruit of an infirmity – on the contrary, it is in order to rediscover the dignity of the human countenance as understood by Stroheim and Dreyer. Now if there is one and only one quality of the silent film irreconcilable by its very nature with sound, it is the syntactical subtlety of montage and expression in the playing of the film, that is to say that which proceeds in effect from the weakness of the silent film. But not all silent films want to be such. Nostalgia for a silence that would be the benign procreator of a visual symbolism unduly confuses the so-called primacy of the image with the true vocation of the cinema – which is the primacy of the object. The absence of a soundtrack for *Greed*, *Nosferatu*, or *La Passion de Jeanne d'Arc* means something quite other than the silence of *Caligari*, *Die Nibelungen*, or *Eldorado*. It is a frustration, not the foundation of a form of expression. The former films exist in spite of their silence not because of it. In this sense the invention of the soundtrack is just a fortuitous scientific phenomenon and not the aesthetic revolution people always say it is. The language of film, like the language of Æsop, is ambiguous and in spite of appearances to the contrary, the history of cinema before and after 1928 is an unbroken continuity. It is the story of the relations between expressionism and realism. Sound was to destroy expressionism for a while before adopting it in its turn. On the other hand, it became an immediate part of the continued development of realism.

Paradoxically enough it is to the most theatrical, that is to say to the most talkative, forms of the sound film that we must look today for a resurgence of the old symbolism while the pre-talkie realism of a Stroheim has in fact no following. Yet, it is evident that Bresson's undertaking is somehow related to the work of Stroheim and Renoir. The separating of sound and of the image to which it relates cannot be understood without a searching examination of the aesthetics of realism in sound. It is just as mistaken to see it as an illustration of a text, as a commentary on an image. Their parallelism maintains that division which is present to our senses. It continues the Bressonian dialectic between abstraction and reality thanks to which we are concerned with a single reality – that of

human souls. In no sense does Bresson return to the expressionism of the silent film. On the one hand he excludes one of the components of reality in order to reproduce it, deliberately stylised on a sound track, partially independent of the image. In other words, it is as if the final re-recording was composed of sound directly recorded with scrupulous fidelity and a text post-synchronised on a monotone. But, as we have pointed out, this text is itself a second reality, a 'cold aesthetic fact'. Its realism is its style, while the style of the image is primarily its reality, and the style of the film is precisely the conflict between the two.

Bresson disposes once and for all of that commonplace of criticism according to which image and sound should never duplicate one another. The most moving moments in the film are those in which text and image are saying the same thing, each however in its own way. The sound never serves simply to fill out what we see. It strengthens it and multiplies it just as the echo chamber of a violin echoes and multiplies the vibrations of the strings. Yet this metaphor is dialectically inadequate since it is not so much a resonance that the mind perceives as something that does not match, as when a colour is not properly superimposed on a drawing. It is here at the edge that the event reveals its true significance. It is because the film is entirely structured on this relationship that, towards the end, the images take on such emotional power. It would be vain to look for its devastating beauty simply in what is explicit. I doubt if the individual frames in any other film, taken separately, are so deceptive. Their frequent lack of plastic composition, the awkwardness and static quality of the actors completely mislead one as to their value in the overall film. Moreover, this accretion of effectiveness is not due to the editing. The value of an image does not depend on what precedes or follows it. They accumulate, rather, a static energy, like the parallel leaves of a condenser. Between this and the soundtrack differences of aesthetic potential are set up, the tension of which becomes unbearable. Thus the image-text relationship moves towards its climax, the latter having the advantage. Thus it is that, quite naturally, at the command of an imperious logic, there is nothing more that the image has to communicate except by disappearing. The spectator has been led, step by step, towards that night of the senses the only expression of which is a light on a blank screen.

That is where the so-called silent film and its lofty realism is headed, to the disappearance of the image and its replacement simply by the text of the novel. But here we are experimenting with an irrefutable aesthetic, with a sublime achievement of pure cinema. Just as the blank page of Mallarmé and the silence of Rimbaud is language at the highest state, the screen, free of images and handed back to literature, is the triumph of cinematographic realism. The black cross on the white screen, as awkwardly drawn as on the average memorial card, the only trace left by the 'assumption' of the image, is a witness to something the reality of which is itself but a sign.

With *Le Journal* cinematographic adaptation reaches a new stage. Up to now, film tended to substitute for the novel in the guise of its aesthetic translation into another language. Fidelity meant respect for the spirit of the novel, but it also meant a search for necessary equivalents, that is to say, it meant taking into account the dramatic requirements of the theatre or again the more direct effectiveness of the cinematographic image. Unfortunately, concern for these things will continue to be the general rule. We must remember however that it was through their application that *Le Diable au corps* and *La Symphonie pastorale* turned out so well. According to the best opinions, films like these are as good as the books on which they are modelled.

In the margin of this formula we might also note the existence of the free adaptation of books such as that made by Renoir for *Une Partie de campagne* or *Madame Bovary*. Here the problem is solved in another way. The original is just a source of inspiration. Fidelity is here the temperamental affinity between film-maker and novelist, a deeply sympathetic understanding. Instead of presenting itself as a substitute, the film is intended to take its place alongside the book – to make a pair with it, like twin stars. This assumption, applicable only where there is genius, does not exclude the possibility that the film is a greater achievement than its literary model, as in the case of Renoir's *The River*.

Le Journal however is something else again. Its dialectic between fidelity and creation is reducible, in the last analysis, to a dialectic between the cinema and literature. There is no question here of a translation, no matter how faithful or intelligent. Still less is it a question of free inspiration with the intention of making a duplicate. It is a question of building a secondary work with the novel as foundation. In no sense is the film 'comparable' to the novel or 'worthy' of it. It is a new aesthetic creation, the novel so to speak multiplied by the cinema.

The only procedure in any way comparable of which we have any examples are films of paintings. Emmer or Alain Resnais are similarly faithful to the original, their raw material is the already highly developed work of the painter; the reality with which they are concerned is not the subject of the painting but the painting itself, in the same way as the text of the novel is Bresson's reality. But the fidelity of Alain Resnais to Van Gogh is but the prior condition of a symbiosis of cinema and painting. That is why, as a rule, painters fail utterly to understand the whole procedure. If you see

Stills: Diary of a Country Priest. *Opposite – Chantal's brother gives the priest a lift on his motor cycle (see also p. 120).*

these films as nothing more than an intelligent, effective, and even a valuable means of popularising painting – they certainly are that too – you know nothing of their aesthetic biology.

This comparison with films of paintings, however, is only partially valid since these are confined from the outset to the realm of minor aesthetic works. They add something to the paintings, they prolong their existence, they release them from the confines of their frames, but they can never pretend to be the paintings themselves. The Van Gogh of Alain Resnais is a minor masterpiece taken from a major *oeuvre* which it makes use of and explains in detail but does not replace. There are two reasons for this congenital limitation. First of all, the photographic reproduction, in projection, cannot pretend to be a substitute for the original or to share its identity. If it could, then it would be the better to destroy its aesthetic autonomy, since films of paintings start off precisely as the negation of that on which this aesthetic autonomy is based, the fact that the paintings are circumscribed in space and exist outside time. It is because cinema as the art of space and time is the contrary of painting that it has something to add to it.

Such a contradiction does not exist between the novel and the film. Not only are they both narrative arts, that is to say temporal arts, but it is not even possible to maintain *a priori* that the cinematic image is essentially inferior to the image prompted by the written word. In all probability the opposite is the case. But this is not where the problem lies. It is enough if the novelist, like the filmmaker, is concerned with the idea of unfolding a real world. Once we accept these essential resemblances, there is nothing absurd in trying to write a novel on film. But *Le Journal* has just proved to us that it is more fruitful to speculate on their differences rather than on their resemblances, that is, for the existence of the novel to be affirmed by the film and not dissolved into it. It is hardly enough to say of this work, once removed, that it is in essence faithful to the original because, to begin with, it *is* the novel. But most of all the resulting work is not, certainly, better (that kind of judgement is meaningless . . .) but 'more' than the book. The aesthetic pleasure we derive from Bresson's film, while the acknowledgement for it goes, essentially, to the genius of Bernanos, includes all that the novel has to offer plus, in addition, its refraction in the cinema.

After Bresson, Aurenche and Bost are but the Viollet-le-Duc of cinematographic adaptation.

UN CONDAMNE A MORT S'EST ECHAPPE

LEO MURRAY

'I would like to show this miracle: an invisible hand over the prison, directing what happens and causing such and such a thing to succeed for one and not for another...The film is a mystery...The Spirit breathes where it will.' (Robert Bresson, cited in *Télérama*, no. 334.)

The film is based on André Devigny's own account of his experience, which was published in *Le Figaro Littéraire* for 20th November, 1954. Imprisoned by the Gestapo for his activities with the French Resistance movement during the German occupation, Devigny managed to escape from Fort Montluc in Lyons just a few hours before he was to have been executed. Bresson placed the following lines at the beginning of his film: 'This story is true. I give it as it is, without embellishment.' Devigny worked closely with Bresson during the filming to ensure accuracy of detail as well as fidelity to the facts. He also expanded his article into a book, which was published by Gallimard in the same year that the film was released. Despite his close adherence to the historical circumstances of Devigny's escape, Bresson has made a film that is entirely personal. He did his own adaptation and dialogue, in this way moving a step further toward becoming the complete author of his film. This is the first film for which he wrote the entire script without any assistance and without taking his dialogue from another source as he had done for *The Diary of a Country Priest*. Bresson likes to talk about Devigny's reaction when he read the script

to him. Upon hearing the dialogue invented by Bresson, Devigny instinctively remarked, *'Comme c'est vrai!'*. The film is also personal because, as Bresson feels, part of his own experience of imprisonment by the Germans went into its making. And then, too, it is personal because of the author's style and because of the view of the world that this style expresses. Claude Monod, who plays the Protestant minister in the film, wrote in *Cahiers du Cinéma* 'During the filming, from evening to evening, at the projection of the rushes, we perceived that this literary fidelity was only a marvellous pretext for Bresson, and that, by means of this "exceptional" adventure, he was composing an "eternal" work to the glory of grace and the will of man.'

In view of the material with which he was working, there were a number of possibilities open to Bresson in making this film. He could have made a documentary on prison life. He could have made a film to the glory of the French Resistance. Or he could have made a suspense-thriller about an escape from prison. In a sense he did all of these and at the same time he did none of them. The Resistance aspect is perhaps the least important in the film. It is an element whose presence is felt, but it is there without any emphasis. It is the simple fact out of which the circumstances of the film grew. Far more important is the documentary side of the film. The value of André Devigny's account of his escape resides chiefly in its authenticity, and it was this authenticity above all that Bresson wanted to preserve. It was for this reason that he insisted on filming in the exact spot where these events happened, and much of the film was shot on location at Fort Montluc in Lyons. For his studio work, Bresson had his technicians construct an exact replica of Devigny's cell and the corridor outside the cell. By an odd coincidence and a singular piece of good fortune (the Spirit breathes where it will?) the actual ropes and hooks that Devigny himself had made and used

Still: Fontaine, the film's Devigny.

were still preserved in Lyons and Bresson used these and Devigny's own help in fashioning the instruments of escape for his film. But despite this concern for authenticity and accuracy of detail, the film is not a documentary about prison life (though it is perhaps a documentary about an escape from prison). It is hardly a complete picture of prison life at all. Everything is presented from the point of view of the protagonist. We never see or hear significantly more than he does and often enough not even as much. While things are happening around him the camera dwells on

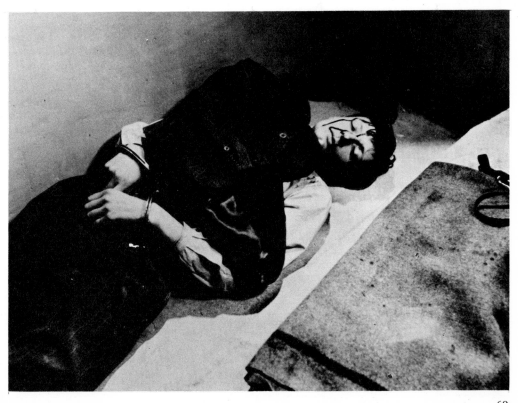

his face. When he looks around his cell, we do not see the cell, and the camera never gives us a general view of it but only shows the parts which are important at any given instant: the window, the door, the cot, the air-vent where Fontaine (the film's equivalent of Devigny) hides his pencil, the walls. The first time he is taken to the court-yard to wash the blood from his face, he looks around, but the camera stays fixed on him. We do not see what he sees but only his reaction to it.

Nor has Bresson made a suspense-thriller about Fontaine's escape although the escape is the subject of his film. Andrew Sarris has attributed the failure of the American critics to understand the film partially to the fact that they expected it to be a suspense-thriller. We know from the start what the outcome of the film will be. The title has already indicated this. And yet there is a certain suspense as we watch Fontaine make his ropes and hooks, as we see him overcome one difficulty only to be faced by another, and finally as we watch his agonised passage over the roof-tops with Jost and his moment of indecision before making the final leap to freedom.

This use and non-use of these three elements may perhaps form another sort of dialectic in the work of Bresson. An analysis of the opening sequence will show how he has made this dialectic work in *A Man Escaped*.

The first image of the film is a shot of a plaque on the wall of Fort Montluc commemorating the prisoners who died there during the occupation. The camera pans to the rough wall of the prison and the credits of the film are superimposed. The film itself begins with a close-up of a man's hands resting on his knees. Cautiously his left hand moves to a car door-handle and discovers that it is not locked. The hand comes back to the knees. The camera pulls back and tilts slightly up to reveal the man's face (it is Fontaine), then pans

left to reveal a second man and then a third. Then it tilts down to show us that the second and third man are hand-cuffed together. It pans back to the face of the first man. We hear vague noises from the street. Cut to a medium shot of the windshield seen between the shoulders of the driver and the guard. Through the windshield we see an almost deserted street in Lyons; the guard's face is partially visible in the rear-view mirror. Close-up of Fontaine and the man beside him, both staring straight ahead. Close-up of the windshield; we see a wagon drawn by two horses. Close-up of Fontaine's face. He glances from the door-handle to the windshield. Close-up of the driver's hand on the gear-shift; he changes gear. Close-up of Fontaine's face; he exchanges a glance with his companion without moving his head. The driver's hand shifting gears. Several rapid cuts from door-handle to Fontaine's face. The windshield, through which we can see that the car is passing the wagon. The three prisoners; Fontaine watches the windshield intently. Through the windshield we see that the car is approaching a bridge, while a trolley is coming from the opposite direction. Close-up of Fontaine and his companion; Fontaine looks from the door-handle to the windshield. The trolley, seen through the windshield, is blocking the way of the car. The driver's hand on the gear-shift. The faces of Fontaine and his companions; Fontaine registers tension and decision. The windshield, again, as the car slows down near the trolley. Another close-up of the faces of Fontaine and his companion; Fontaine suddenly opens the car door and jumps out, moving out of the frame; the camera pulls slightly back and frames the rear of the car including the open door through which Fontaine has escaped and his two companions who sit motionless and impassive, staring ahead; through the open door we see the driver running after Fontaine; through the rear window we see another car stop and several men get out and run after Fontaine. The camera remains fixed, and all the action takes place outside the frame. After a few seconds Fontaine comes back into the frame, enters the car and takes his place. He is handcuffed, and the guard hits him over the head with the handle of a gun. The image dissolves to the courtyard of Fort Montluc.

The entire sequence is composed of about two dozen shots, mostly close-ups and extremely brief. Bresson has said, 'It was a question of making a rapid film with slow things, with the oppressive life of the prison.' The rapid cutting from one brief close-up to another creates a tension and a suspense from the start. Fontaine's will to escape as well as his hesitancy are evident from the opening shot where his hand moves cautiously to the door to see if it can be opened. In a sense, the entire film is going to be nothing more than an elaboration of this brief opening shot. Fontaine's decision is made then and there, and in the succeeding shots as he glances from the door-handle to the windshield we see him looking for the right moment to make his move. The camera searches his face in close-up while he is evidently trying to confirm his decision and steel his will for action.

Bresson's characteristic understatement has perhaps never been so effective as in this film. In this opening sequence the one shot of some duration comes when Fontaine tries to escape. The camera does not follow him. We see nothing of the action in the street outside the car. We hear the noises of whistles, of cars stopping, of running feet and of unintelligible shouting, and we know that inevitably Fontaine will be brought back to the empty seat upon which the camera remains fixed. This sort of ellipsis occurs twice more in the film, again at moments of violence. When Fontaine arrives

Still: Fontaine (François Leterrier).

at the prison we see him taken through a doorway; one of the guards picks up a shovel and follows him. The image dissolves to the same scene, but now Fontaine is being carried out after being beaten. At the end of the film, when Fontaine kills the sentinel, he hides behind a wall waiting for the man to come near. He jumps out of frame and the camera stays fixed on the wall. The sound of the action is covered by the noise of a passing train. After a few seconds Fontaine comes back into the

frame and signals Jost to come down. As they move off from the wall, the camera pulls back just enough to let us see the gun and part of the dead soldier's body. Jost turns to look at him and then follows Fontaine.

By this understatement Bresson avoids anything like sensationalism and at the same time cuts out everything inessential to his purpose. The film is about the will of Fontaine to escape and the Providence of God which allows things to work together in such a way as to permit him to do so. This double theme is evident from the start. The title of the film

Un Condamné à mort s'est échappé (A man condemned to death escaped), is immediately followed by the film's second title *Le Vent souffle où il veut* (The Spirit breathes where it will), the words of Jesus to Nicodemus in the third chapter of Saint John's Gospel. This title forms part of the text that the Protestant Minister later gives Fontaine to read. Bresson had wanted to use this as the title of the film but was forced to accept the actual title by the producers. Originally he had wanted to put the two ideas of Fontaine's will to escape and God's Providence into a single title by simply calling

Stills: Fontaine at work on his cell door.

the film *Aide-toi* which is part of a French dictum ('*Aide-toi, le ciel t'aidera*') whose English equivalent is 'Heaven helps him who helps himself'. With the titles we hear the music of the 'Kyrie' from Mozart's Mass in C Minor, which will recur at certain specific moments during the film.

In the opening sequence, the main visual themes of the film are established; Fontaine's hands, which will fashion the instruments of escape, and his face, to which the camera constantly returns. Another theme that is suggested here by the door-handle and the driver's hand on the gear-shift is the role of material objects in the film, especially as they contribute in their own way to Fontaine's escape; the spoon that he uses to dismantle his door, his cot, the blankets, and the wire that we see transformed into the instruments of escape. Eric Rohmer entitled his review of the film in *Cahiers du Cinéma*, 'The miracle of objects'; 'Everything in the film can be explained naturally . . . yet with all the difficulties we are led to say the word *miracle*. Everything is grace, to which Bresson adds, ". . . even free will and human patience," ' and we might also add, even the most insignificant acts and the countless material objects of daily life. Bresson underlines this conviction by having the music of Mozart's Mass accompany the emptying of the slop-buckets in the courtyard.

In his account of his escape André Devigny had written, 'There were two parts in it, mine and God's. Where was the limit ? I did not know but I felt that heaven would cast its glance upon this deaf and resolute struggle only to the extent that I would put the most hidden of my physical and moral resources into the balance.' It was this perhaps that suggested the original title to Bresson. But in fact he has actually gone far beyond the rather mechanistic, *quid pro quo* concept of Providence expressed by '*Aide-toi, le ciel t'aidera*.' His Fontaine is obviously not a pious man, but he is a believer. He tells the Minister that he prays; he reads the text from Saint John with respect and interest, and just before his escape he asks a priest who is also a prisoner to pray for him. But at the same time, he can also say, 'It would be too good if God took care of everything,' and he goes about his work as if God had no part in it at all. Yet part of the meaning of the film is that God is very much involved in everything that happens, and that, knowingly or unknowingly, willingly or unwillingly, we are all parts of some higher plan, which in no way diminishes our individual liberty. Quite the contrary. Fontaine's obsession with escaping, his passion for freedom, his compulsion to struggle against the forces that oppress him, make him a very contemporary figure. He is constantly creating his own freedom and in this sense is constantly asserting himself as a man. (A comparison with some of Sartre's ideas on freedom might be interesting here.) When Blanchet, the old man in the next cell, questioning him about his obstinacy, asks, 'Why all that ?' he simply answers, 'To

struggle.' Working on his door, he says, 'This door had to open . . . I had foreseen nothing for afterwards.' Blanchet asks him, 'You are going to get out ? How will you do it ?'. Fontaine answers, 'I swear I have no idea.' He sees a value simply in the struggle, in the will not to give in.

This dual theme of the will of Fontaine to escape and the Providence of God that permits him to escape is translated cinematically by the alternance of scenes in which Fontaine is alone and scenes with the other prisoners. In the privacy of his own cell he devises his plan for escape and there, too, he transforms spoons into knives, blankets into ropes and lanterns into hooks, apparently without reflecting upon the possible absurdity of the work he is doing. This transformation is presented by a series of dissolves which show the hands of Fontaine, the instrument and sign of his will, accomplishing this quasi-miracle – for so it seems as the ropes and hooks take shape before our eyes. The construction of the film counterpoints these scenes with those showing Fontaine in contact with the other prisoners. Bresson chose a very curious yet highly effective way of translating Fontaine's relations with the other prisoners. We never see them until Fontaine has actually managed to communicate with them or at least has the desire to do so. The first time he goes to the courtyard, he looks around but we do not see what he sees. We see others only as they begin to have a meaningful relation to Fontaine. His first contact with Terry is going to enable him to communicate with the outside world. When he goes down to the courtyard after tapping on the wall and getting no response from Blanchet, the only other person we see is Blanchet. As the other prisoners enter the world of Fontaine our own vision of his surroundings becomes enlarged. We see more of the washroom as we get to know more of the prisoners and as more of them become interested in Fontaine and in his escape. A solidarity is established between him and the others as they aid each other with mutual encouragement and advice. What is exterior to Fontaine is interesting only to the extent that it provokes a reaction in him and it is only to this extent that the spectator is allowed to see it. Once again the value of Bresson's film resides to a large extent in its portrayal of an interior state.

Still: in the courtyard, Fontaine and (left) the minister (Roland Monod).

I have said that the theme of Providence is more obvious in the scenes relating Fontaine to the other prisoners. Providence here might just as easily be called chance or coincidence and one could see and enjoy the film without even reflecting on the possibility of some '... invisible hand over the prison directing what happens and causing such and such a thing to succeed for one and not for another.' Bresson himself, as his statement implies, and as much of what we have seen in the film indicates, would perhaps deny that there is such a thing as chance. He seems to be saying that what

appears as accident or coincidence is really part of another scheme of things. Bresson has said in *Cahiers du Cinéma*:

'What you have just called mysticism must come from what I feel in a prison, that is, as the second title *Le Vent souffle où il veut* indicates, those extraordinary currents, the presence of something or someone, call it what you will, that directs everything like a hand. Prisoners are very sensitive to this curious atmosphere, which is in no way a dramatic atmosphere; it all happens on a level that is much higher. You hear people being executed but no one raises an eye-brow; it's normal; it's part of prison life. All the drama is interior.'

Orsini's failure in his attempt to escape alone makes Fontaine's escape possible since without the information that Orsini gives him Fontaine could never have got out. The first time Orsini speaks to Fontaine, he says to him, 'Take me with you.' Back in his cell, Fontaine looks through the peep-hole of his door and watches Orsini entering his own cell. Then he sees the guard open the ventilator in the

Still: Jost and Fontaine.

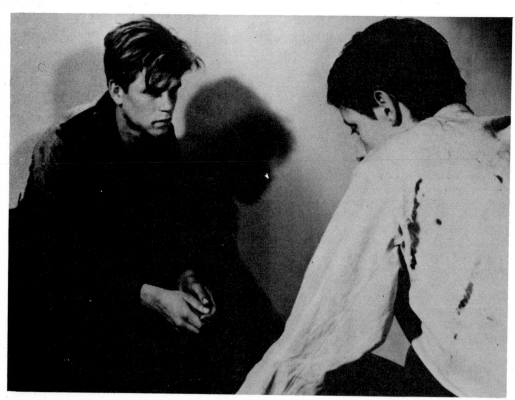

ceiling. His attention is drawn for the first time to the skylight as a possible route to freedom. In the washroom Fontaine places a note in the pocket of the Minister's jacket which is hanging with a number of others while the prisoners perform their ablutions. As it happens, on that particular day, the ·guard decides to search the pockets of the prisoners, but when he comes to the Minister's jacket and sees the tiny cross on the lapel, he passes it by without searching it. The Minister simply says, 'Mon Dieu!' Earlier in the film, the Minister, who had asked Fontaine if he had a Bible, finds one in the pocket of his coat. How it got there is not explained. Fontaine says, 'It's a miracle.' The Minister replies, 'I was lucky.' Then as the Minister walks out of the frame, the camera follows Fontaine to a ledge in the washroom. Fontaine says, 'I was lucky, too,' and picks up a spoon lying there; it replaces the one he had been using and which had broken.

The cells are searched after the prisoners have been ordered to hand in all pencils. The guard arrives to search Fontaine's cell at the same time that Fontaine receives a package from home. Instead of searching his cell for the pencil (the discovery of which could have meant the prisoner's immediate execution), the guard simply looks through the package and leaves. Even the arrival of Jost, who seems to upset Fontaine's plans completely, proves to be an element in facilitating his escape. In fact without Jost's help he could not have scaled the second wall. Fontaine remarks, 'Alone, I could perhaps have gone no farther.' His instinct had inclined him in the right direction when he decided not to kill Jost, but to take him with him.

The idea of solidarity among the prisoners, of mutual aid and encouragement, becomes intermingled with the notion of providence. This is particularly evident in the relationship between Fontaine and the Protestant Minister and in the developing friendship between Fontaine and Blanchet. The role of the Minister in the film is to remind us of the part played by God in these events. Not that his role is contrived. On the contrary. There actually was a Protestant Minister in prison with Devigny with whom he became very friendly and who actually did copy a text from Scripture and give it to Devigny, encouraging him to pray. The text, however, was not the one that is used in the film but rather the following, 'Ask and you shall receive, seek and you shall find, knock and it shall be opened to you.' Bresson's changing the text is in accord with his rights as an adaptor and a 'metteur-en-ordre' and is consistent with the meaning of the film. In a conversation that curiously parallels the one between Jesus and Nicodemus, the Minister tells Fontaine that he must have hope, that hope is a kind of life, and that this must be part of what Jesus meant by his words to Nicodemus. Later in the film he hands Fontaine a paper on which he has copied the text from Saint John's Gospel.

Blanchet at first refuses to recognise or speak to Fontaine until Fontaine helps him in the courtyard when he faints. And even then his response is curt and cynical. He had been imprisoned for possessing some dollars entrusted to him by a Jewish woman whom he had never seen before. He is bitter and despairing, but in the course of his conversations his attitude changes. He becomes sympathetic towards Fontaine and his plan for escape. Through Blanchet, the text from Saint John is put in direct relationship to the death of Orsini and the escape of Fontaine. At the moment when Orsini is executed – this fact is communicated to the viewer, as well as to Fontaine and Blanchet, by the sound of a machine gun – Fontaine is reading the text to Blanchet who then says to him: 'Orsini had to fail so that you could succeed.' The rest of the

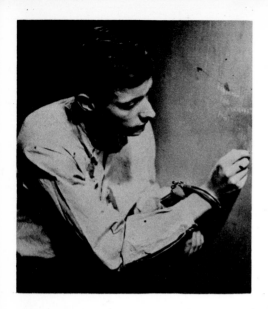

dialogue here is also interesting for the way it reveals the evolution in Blanchet's character as well as a certain sensitivity in Fontaine. Fontaine answers: 'That's extraordinary.' Blanchet: 'I'm telling you nothing you don't already know.' Fontaine: 'What's extraordinary, Monsieur Blanchet, is that it is you who say it.' Symbolically, Fontaine will receive 'new life,' his freedom, when he escapes and at the same time he restores hope to Blanchet who even co-operates actively in the escape by giving him his blanket. In fact Fontaine becomes a symbol of hope for all the prisoners. Recall that the Minister had found the notion of hope implied in the idea of life in the words of Jesus to Nicodemus. When Fontaine says goodbye to Blanchet, the old man simply answers, '*Adieu, mon ami.*'

One would say that a prison is a place *par excellence* of solitude. What is remarkable about this film is that the prisoners, though physically separated, are in constant communication. The signs of this communication are the sack that Fontaine lets down outside his window, the tapping on the walls, the glances exchanged in the corridors, the furtive conversations, the notes passed in the washroom, Fontaine and Blanchet at their cell-windows. Most important of all is the music because it adds a new meaning to this communication. It raises it to the higher level of communication. We hear the 'Kyrie' from Mozart's Mass at the very beginning of the film. It recurs seven times during the course of the film; three times as the prisoners descend to the courtyard to empty their slop-buckets, once when Orsini attempts his escape, again when he is taken from his cell to be executed, and again when Jost arrives and Fontaine must decide whether to kill him or to take him on the escape. At the end of the film it returns again as Fontaine and Jost walk off in the night, free men. In this way the music becomes a sign of Providence (its use behind the title, *Le Vent souffle où il veut*, with Orsini's attempted escape and his execution, with the arrival of Jost and at the moment of success) as well as of communion. The choir is heard singing 'Lord, have mercy' only three times: at the beginning of the film, as Orsini tries to escape, and at the very end. In the other instances we hear the orchestra, still playing the 'Kyrie' but without the voices. Sémolué suggests that this final 'Kyrie eleison' is a thanksgiving for the escape, but retains what he calls its 'sorrowful' aspect: '...the appeal persists for all those who remain behind the walls that have been scaled by Fontaine, whether they be prisoners or jailers; the appeal to mercy then even seems to concern, beyond the prisoners, the entire human race.' Henri Agel speaks of the Communion of Saints in this context and says it is impossible to understand the film without reference to this dimension.

This is the first time that Bresson has been completely successful in his use of music, which is used very sparingly, just a few bars, to add a certain rhythm at the moments when it occurs. Bresson himself has said that the 'colour' of this music seemed to him to be the 'colour' of the film. It is striking to see how perfectly Mozart's music accompanies the emptying of the buckets and at the same time gives a new depth of meaning to this banal action. As Sémolué says, '... it recalls that the simplest facts hide and reveal the execution of a secret design. It indicates that through visible actions another action is unfolding whose sense can escape us but which none-theless directs us. Through the truth of the reality that the whole film shows us, the music establishes the reality of Truth; or at least it sets up the conditions under which this can be seen.'

As usual in Bresson's films, all the elements of the sound track are very important. Besides the music, there is a commentary-off spoken by Fontaine. As in *Diary of a Country Priest*, it is in the past, while what we see is in the present, thus in a sense destroying real time and re-fashioning it for the purposes of the film. Despite certain specific references to time, especially toward the end of the film, what happens here is almost a-temporal, as in *Les Dames du Bois de Boulogne*. This is perhaps a characteristic of prison life. If so, Bresson has captured it perfectly. At the same time it is perfectly consistent with and in a sense flows from the deeper meaning of his film. (Once again, it is impossible to separate form from content, or the form creates a meaning beyond that of the original material, which was the escape of Devigny.) On the other hand, the commentary here seems to me to be less successful than in *Diary of a Country Priest*. It adds a certain rhythm which becomes an additional element in the composition of the

film, but at the same time one has the impression that Bresson relies perhaps a little too heavily on it to keep his film moving. This is a minor fault and one that Bresson himself recognises. He says that if he were to make the film today, he would do it without the commentary.

Natural sound has its part to play in the film as well – and an important one at that. In fact – and this seems to be becoming a characteristic of Bresson's aesthetic of the cinema – the sound seems even more important than the image, never simply supporting or explaining or reinforcing it, except sometimes in the case of the commentary, but rather adding a meaning that the image itself does not convey. Bresson himself has said that, properly used, the music and sound of a film can transport us into a region that is no longer simply terrestrial, but rather, cosmic, ' . . . I would even say divine.'

Although the prison is cut off from the outside world, this world is continually present in the sounds that the prisoners hear: the trains that are constantly passing, the trolley with its bell, the voices of people beyond the walls. Once again the evocative power of sound in the cinema can be seen as a powerful means of suggesting a whole world beyond what we see on the screen. The prison is not the whole of reality and even the prisoners are not permitted to think so as the sounds of the world outside break in upon their solitude.

The sounds we hear from inside the prison itself assume the quality of signs. These may be signs of menace (the creaking bicycle of the guard who rides around the prison walls at the end of the film), of presence (the rattling of the guard's key on the metal bannister), of communication (the tapping on the walls between prison cells), of death (the machine-gun).

This last sound brings me to the idea of death that haunts this film. Death is present from the beginning to the end. But this is a presence that is felt rather than seen, like the invisible hand over the prison directing what happens there. Fontaine himself escapes death – or at least he thinks so – at the beginning by pretending he cannot walk. His comrade in the cell on the ground floor, a man whom he had never seen, is executed and he himself is deeply affected by this. Orsini also must die so that he, Fontaine, can escape. From time to time we hear the sound of machine-guns communicating the fact of an execution. It is the news of his own condemnation that finally moves Fontaine to action. He contemplates killing Jost and finally he does kill the sentinel, the last major obstacle between himself and freedom.

This unseen but threatening presence of death is particularly impressive at the moment of Orsini's execution. We hear the sound of the machine-gun. Its rat-tat-tat carries over into what Bresson calls the 'harmonics' of the next image, which begins in absolute silence. Bresson says that Orsini's death is in that silence; and then Fontaine begins to dismantle the lantern in his cell to make the hooks. If death is in the silence, it is also in the movement in the image and in its significance. This is by far the most dangerous thing that Fontaine has yet attempted: to alter the external appearance of his cell. If this were discovered, the consequences would be grave. And yet he must take the risk. It is Orsini's death that pushes him to this brink.

Fontaine is seeking to escape from death as much as from the prison. In a sense it is this constant threat of death that motivates him, the desire to live almost as much as the desire to be free.

Perhaps it is this particular aspect of the film that has led one critic to ask: 'Do these people possess true spiritual light? Does their will direct them toward the only authentic ends? When the two finally cross the last wall, they disappear into the night. Toward what end? Could Bresson answer this question?' (Jean d'Yvoire in *Radio-Cinéma-Télévision*). One is strongly tempted to reply, 'Does it make any difference whether Bresson could answer the question or not?'. The question is in fact quite irrelevant to the film and its meaning. This sort of writing, though obviously sincere and frequently quite intelligent, is unfortunately typical of a certain kind of 'Catholic' criticism, which, in its anxiety to preserve orthodoxy and traditional Christian morality, will sometimes step aside from the point at issue. It is interesting to note that non-Catholic critics, less concerned about orthodoxy, can sometimes be more objective and accurate in their evaluations of a film like this with religious overtones. Jean d'Yvoire asks if the film is really a resurrection. The answer is that it *is* a resur-

rection in the sense that life comes from death, at least figuratively if not literally. There is even a certain causal relationship between Orsini's death and Fontaine's escape. Life within the prison is really a sort of non-life and from this Fontaine is reborn into the new life of freedom. This is obviously not the resurrection of Christ, nor perhaps (and that 'perhaps' is an important one) does it have an eschatological significance, but the fact remains

Still: carrying ropes they have made out of blankets, Fontaine and Jost escape.

that the film presents a mystery, one that has puzzled theologians for centuries and has been the object of bitter controversy: the freedom of man and the Providence of God. Since Bresson is not a theologian, he does not attempt to explain or justify this mystery. We might simply say that he celebrates it.

PICKPOCKET

DANIEL MILLAR

Pickpocket is an exception among Bresson's films, which mostly seem to exist in isolation from the rest of the cinematic world, faithful only to a text and to the director's vision and style – Bresson claims to see few films, though the editors of *Cahiers de Cinéma* dispute this. Here there is no pre-existing text, although the relationship between Michel and the police Inspector has well-known affinities with *Crime and Punishment*. But the similarity of the early Métro scenes to those of another pickpocket (Richard Widmark) on the subway in Samuel Fuller's *Pickup on South Street* (1953) almost looks like an *hommage* and surely suggests a possible source of topic (though, curiously, the film was not shown in France till 1961); while the effect of Hitchcock's most (indeed, only) Bressonian and quasi-documentary film, *The Wrong Man* (1957), may possibly appear in the casting as Michel of Martin Lassalle, who resembles a younger Henry Fonda. Less disputably, *Pickpocket* itself has influenced several Nouvelle Vague directors including Godard, notably in *Le Petit Soldat*, and Démy in his least characteristic but arguably his best film, *Baie des Anges*.

If the French descendants seem less surprising than the American ancestors, this is partly because *Pickpocket* has acquired the reputation of a difficult, austere film – for Louis Malle, an allegory of the Fall and Redemption of Man; for the hostile critics of *Positif*, another crazed step towards the empty screen posited as the ultimate Bresson image by André Bazin. Bresson's opening disclaimer that the film is not a thriller, seems in such a climate scarcely necessary – and, some might add, an under-statement. In England the general consensus was that Bresson had gone a bit too far this time. In retrospect it ought by now to be clearer that, if he ever did go too far, it was in *Procès de Jeanne d'Arc* rather than *Pickpocket* and that if he has made a specially difficult film, it is *Balthazar*, not *Pickpocket*. For *Pickpocket* is a fairly simple and generally successful film, somewhat slighter than its two predecessors, which seems difficult mainly because of some stylistic originalities and a few ellipses in action. That it took only ten months from conception to Paris opening – compared with the long years that went into *Balthazar* and the still unrealised *Lancelot du Lac* – suggests a relatively straightforward, though not superficial, basic pattern.

One common error has been the search for hidden depths of psychology, maybe inspired by the parallel with Dostoievsky. Michel's relationship with his mother has been a favourite area for probing, since he refuses to see her until she is seriously ill – in fact, dying – and then expresses affection for her. From here it is a short Freudian step to the Inspector as friendly yet rejected father-figure, and then to the gestures of theft as surreptitious carresses, so that Michel's final declaration of love for Jeanne becomes his ultimate renunciation of his repressed homosexuality. This sort of over-interpretation ignores not only Bresson's statement that he dislikes psychology and tries not to use it, but also the clear story-line of the

film itself. Michel's behaviour is meant to seem puzzling and inconsistent – until we learn that he stole from his mother a year before. He himself does not know the full story until he pieces it together from the Inspector and Jeanne after his mother's death – it is that she had made a complaint of theft to the police and then, presumably guessing the culprit, withdrawn it. In the light of this, the opening of the film, at Longchamp, is clearer – the theft from a woman, when most of his later victims are men; the arrest on suspicion and the release; giving some of the stolen money to Jeanne for

Still: Michel at work in the Métro.

his mother, but refusing to go in and face her. His violent heart-beats at the act of theft mark not quasi-sexual excitement but a key moment of choice and self-discovery, a choice of evil – just as his heart-beats when he receives Jeanne's letter in prison, near the end, signal his relief that she has not abandoned him after all and his realisation that she, not suicide, is his solution. Michel does find theft more exciting than work and he has a streak of kleptomania about watches – but these seem fairly typical qualities, even qualifications, for a professional pickpocket.

If the psychology is direct, unobscure and relatively naturalistic, so is the spiritual drama. Jeanne will not really stand up as a modern Beatrice, still less as a female Jesus, and her illegitimate child by Jacques should be enough to make it clear that she is not so intended. To see her as a mixture of Balthazar and Marie, or even to compare her with Madeleine in *Les*

Still: Michel with the pickpocket (Kassagi) who teaches him the skills of the trade.

Parapluies de Cherbourg, might be nearer the right level. Similarly, the nameless pickpockets played by Kassagi and Pierre Etaix are certainly villains, but not devils. In fact, there is a certain amount of honour and even wordless camaraderie among thieves, and their practice of their trade, particularly at the Gare de Lyon, is dazzlingly skilful – though this remains the charm of evil, and culminates in their ignominious arrest. Neither appears to repent, so it is not necessary to get over-excited by recollection of Jesus's two flanking thieves – anyway, when Michel does acquire some ironic stigmata

by falling down in the course of stealing a gold watch, he is strictly without his accomplices since, appropriately, it is a Sunday and he is out at a fair in Neuilly with Jeanne and Jacques.

Even so, the possibility that Michel functions as a sort of reversed mirror-image of the *curé de campagne* need not be dismissed out of hand – and is even reinforced by Bresson's decision to invent a written text for Michel, since none already existed. Certainly this '*journal d'un pickpocket de ville*', of which we hear much more than we see, is nearer a spiritual confession than a legal statement, though naturally without the references to God and to movements of the soul which occupy much of the curé's attention. In fact, the spiritual values are neatly reversed – the stolen gold watch is '*très belle*'; or, of the successful thieving session at the Gare de Lyon, '*C'était trop beau. Cela ne pouvait pas durer.*' On this pattern, the two experienced pickpockets occupy for Michel an equivalent position of training and support to the curé of Torcy and Dr Delbende for the curé of Ambricourt; the humble, patient Jeanne matches the proud, scheming Chantal; the ambiguous friendship of the powerful Inspector parallels that of the comte; old women die – Michel's mother and the comtesse; a young friend changes for the worse (Jacques), or for the better (Dufréty, the defrocked ex-seminarian). The analogy would become merely schematic if pushed too hard, and its purpose is only to suggest how *Pickpocket* can be regarded as a spiritual drama of the secular world without pushing it into arid allegory on the one hand or naïve sermonising on the other. Though Bresson's intentions are undoubtedly religious, this need not prevent the agnostic/humanist/Marxist/etc. from finding it meaningful in his own terms, *Positif* notwithstanding.

The most profitable line forward here will be in investigation of style. For Bresson the true cinema is *écriture*, not *spectacle*, so style is the index of truth and a rigorous realism the only possible style. (Hopefully, definitions of realism may differ less than definitions of reality.) Stylistically, *Pickpocket* develops more from *Condamné* than *Journal*, not surprisingly: the same emphasis on still, contained faces and moving, skilled hands, practising and working; the stark, spare beauty of functionally composed and newsreel-textured photography; the punctuations and interactions of commentary and of classical music. Both Fontaine and Michel are labouring illegally, which may explain some of the similarities. Though the

audience accepts without question Fontaine's assumption that he is fighting against an evil régime, it is notable that the pickpockets' victims are presented with little enough sympathy – so neutrally as to seem almost hostile, though admittedly somewhat less so than the German guards at Montluc. This may be Bresson's balance between the abstract proposition of evil and the concrete presentation of Michel's absorbed involvement. Or it may even be the outcome of the difficult shooting conditions involved in the project. For in some respects *Pickpocket* is more original than *Condamné*, even if finally less intense, less impressive.

Bresson used improvisation more than ever before – it was more possible because of the lack of a fixed story, and more necessary in capturing a realistic depiction of the topic. In addition, he was shooting in the streets, stations, cafés of Paris after two provincial excursions – he has since preferred the provinces again. As it happened, he was also level with the young vanguard – the crews of *Pickpocket* and of *A Bout de Souffle* could easily have bumped into each other between 17 August, 1959 (Godard's first day) and 10 September (Bresson's last). And certainly

Pickpocket was more contemporary than any preceding Bresson film – which may be why it appears to have had more direct influence. Bresson's passion for authenticity, shared in less rarefied form by Godard, at least matches that of any documentarist and provides a solid protection against his flying-off to a religious empyrean where only fellow-believers can follow him – which, of course, is precisely the accusation that the *a-bressonistes* level at each succeeding film.

The rigour and yet flexibility of this style is particularly clear in the Gare de Lyon sequence, the part of the film that everyone remembers and virtually a documentary on pickpockets' methods (the theory of which Kassagi had demonstrated in an ealier sequence). As Godard and Doniol-Valcroze have pointed out, it is full of almost invisible travelling shots, not noticed in casual viewing because the concentration is on the manner and sequence of gestures, not on the viewpoint (analogous to watching well-presented sport on television). Less obvious examples abound: the dissolve from the two policemen behind Michel after his first Longchamp theft to all three in the police car; the dissolve from Michel assuring his mother that she will get better to the singing of '*Dies Irae*' at the Requiem Mass (an effect used more extensively in *Balthazar*, e.g. Arnold's decision to give up drinking, immediately broken); the reflection of the fair at Neuilly in the café's window and the dissolve between the empty table as Michel leaves and (same shot, same angle, possibly different take) the empty table as Jeanne and Jacques return. Final example: the pickpocket's gesture with which Michel puts his own rail ticket in his own pocket as he leaves on his two years' exile.

The care in the scenario matches that in *mise en scène*. For instance, Michel meets the Inspector five times: twice at a café with Jacques, once in the Inspector's office, once in

*Stills: pickpocket gestures – removing a watch
(opposite) and replacing a ticket (above).*

his own room, once at Longchamp – each time
a step nearer his ultimate capture. His career
begins and ends at Longchamp. Why? The
police set a trap for him with an *agent-provo-
cateur*. Why there? It is the only place at
which he has been arrested, and the Inspector
has seen him there before his two-year disappearance (no-one seems to notice his activities
at the Gare de Lyon). Fate and naturalism need
no elaborate reconciliation. Of Jeanne's two

letters (and letters are often important in
Bresson's films), the first – about the mother's
illness – is overlooked because Michel is too
obsessed with improving his professional skills;
the second is delayed as Jeanne is too concerned with her baby's illness to visit him in
prison. But such examples of planning and
realisation may well convince only those
already convinced, who will readily find more
for themselves.

Even more controversial than these aspects
has been the problem of casting, particularly
Martin Lassalle's Michel. My own view is that,

87

as casting is so integral an element in Bresson's style, even a slight mistake like Florence Carrez's Jeanne d'Arc is so unmistakeable as to need no debate. Michel is not the same kind of hero as the curé or Fontaine, so it is irrelevant to expect another Claude Laydu or François Leterrier. Martin Lassalle's shifts, waverings, uncertainties, resorts to rhetoric, empty-eyed evasions, add up to a Michel who spends the whole film discovering his true self, who therefore exists only *after* the end of the film. Marika Green as Jeanne is actually more surprising, a pretty, late-'fifties sex-kitten

disciplined to Bressonian enunciation, looks and movements; yet the tension is quite expressive, for Michel is unable to realise that he loves her as long as he is caught up in restless movement, yet unable to resist this conclusion once he arrives at stillness.

Some final comment must be made on the relationship of *Pickpocket* to Bresson's other films, and its place in his work. For a decade, from *Journal* to *Procès*, Bresson explored the character of the Prisoner who seeks and finds Release – in death, escape or, here paradoxically, behind bars. Like Hélène, Chantal and

Still: Michel (Martin Lassalle) and Jeanne (Marika Green) in Pickpocket.

even perhaps Orsini in *Condamné*, Michel makes erroneous choices of which he is proud – yet, like Marie in *Balthazar* and Arsène in *Mouchette*, he retains some good possibilities even while preferring evil. Similarly, Jeanne resembles Agnès and Mlle Louise, the governess, before her as well as Marie and Mouchette after her, in falling into sexual error without thereby destroying her essential moral character and her quality of victim.

In the general picture of Bresson's career, *Pickpocket* has generally and not unreasonably been regarded as falling into the relative trough between the earlier masterpieces, *Journal* and *Condamné*, and the later heights of *Balthazar* and *Mouchette*. Yet it seems to me one of his most intensely characteristic and original exploratory films, and even something of a test-piece. A film-goer who still finds it unrewarding at second or third viewing may happen to enjoy some of Bresson's other films – but it will probably not be for their specifically Bressonian virtues.

LE PROCES DE JEANNE D'ARC

LEO MURRAY

Except for the life of Christ, perhaps no other subject has been filmed as often as the story of Joan of Arc. (Cf. the Filmography established by Vincent Pinel in *Jeanne d'Arc à l'écran, Etudes Cinématographiques*, no. 18-19.) Fittingly enough the first such film was made in France, in 1898 by Georges Hatot. The most recent, also made in France by Francis Lacassin, is a documentary which utilises the papers and engravings about Joan from the fifteenth century in the National Libraries of Paris and of Lyons. Between the two a variety of directors, including Cecil B. DeMille, Victor Fleming, Roberto Rossellini and Otto Preminger have given us their versions of the life of the Maid of Orléans. These films range in style from crassly commercial vehicles for certain Hollywood stars of the silent screen to the awesome and moving meditation on Joan's Passion by Carl Theodore Dreyer, from the lavish, historical study of Victor Fleming, to Bresson's coldly ascetic reconstruction of the trial. The opera singer Geraldine Farrar, fresh from her success as Carmen, played *Joan the Woman* for Cecil B. DeMille who was making his first epic film in 1917. Rossellini filmed Claudel's oratorio, '*Jeanne au bûcher*' with music by Arthur Honegger and Preminger adapted Shaw's play, 'Joan of Arc'. After this long history of successes, half-successes and downright failures, all based on the same subject, Robert Bresson was risking a great deal in taking up once more the story of Joan of Arc. But in spite of all this he has managed to make a film that is entirely original and entirely personal. It is also perhaps the most authentic portrait of Joan that the cinema has given us to date.

There is a very close connection between these two elements of originality and authenticity. The film is based rigorously on the historical record of Joan's trial and of the rehabilitation process twenty-five years later. The austerity and simplicity of the film, as well as the use of non-professionals, by now well recognised characteristics of Bresson's style, almost give it a look of documentary.

In the opening shot, the camera precedes three people – Joan's mother, supported by her two sons – who are walking down the aisle of a Church. It is in fact Notre Dame de Paris, but this is not at all evident from what we see. At the same time, the camera is tilted down to their feet so that we never see their faces. As they arrive at the choir, the camera pulls back to let them pass and we see the prelates who are waiting. The three kneel and Joan's mother reads the formal request for her daughter's rehabilitation. As she reaches the final words, ' . . . they falsely and lyingly imputed numerous crimes to her; finally they vilely condemned her and burned her', we hear a drum roll, a dry, staccato sound like the noise of a machine gun. The credits of the film are run over this same image of Joan's mother, her back to the camera. The drum roll is repeated and this, plus a brief fanfare of trumpets before the first interrogation, is the only music in the film.

And yet, despite this absence of music, one has the impression of a very musical film,

Still: The Trial of Joan of Arc.

musical at least in the sense of rhythmical. The various rhythms are very carefully orchestrated: the rhythm of question and answer in the interrogation scenes; the rhythm of the montage, cutting back and forth from Joan to her examiners, which corresponds to the rhythm of question and answer; a larger rhythm, balancing the formal interrogations against the scenes in Joan's cell which are linked together by the constant ascent and descent of the tower stairway; the rhythm of the French voices with the strange counterpoint of the English voices; the rhythm of the natural sounds, mostly footsteps and doors opening and closing, the grinding of a key in a lock, the clanking of prisoner's chains, occasionally a dog barking in the distance. Bresson has said, 'I tried to render the rhythm of the text like a musical score.'

'The problem was that of a film entirely in questions and in answers. But I was content to use the monotony like a unified background upon which the nuances would be clearly sketched. I had more to fear from the slowness, the heaviness of the trial. So I attack the film

and continue it in very rapid rhythm. One can write a film with quavers and semi-quavers because there is music in it. The cinematographer is not there, nor is the film, to copy life, but to catch us up in a rhythm of which the author must remain the master.' (Interview with Jean Guitton in *Etudes Cinématographiques*.)

As the first interrogation begins, we at first see only Joan's hands on the book of the Gospels while she swears to tell the truth. The camera then frames her in medium shot and remains fixed through a series of short questions about her life. Only at the end of this interro-

Stills: The interrogation of Joan of Arc.

gation when the Bishop speaks of his authority does the camera cut to a medium shot of him. In succeeding interrogations the editing follows the back and forth movement of the questions and answers. Each interrogation takes up more or less the same matter, but each time Joan's answers reveal a little more about her than they did before. This is another element in the rhythm of the film, like a theme that is taken up in turn and further elaborated by the different sections of an orchestra. Bresson deliberately chose the replies that would emphasise the spiritual aspect of his heroine and her interior struggle. In so doing he also deliberately made the images of his film, at least in the interrogations, subordinate to the words. 'My film was born of words, was constructed from words. My film is in questions and in answers for it was in this form that the interrogations were registered.' (Interview with Yvonne Baby in *Le Monde*.) To some critics this seemed like a contradiction, an anti-cinema, while others saw it as a break-through in film-style. Beginning with *The Diary of a Country Priest*, Bresson has tended to give more and more value to the text. This is a stylistic device that was at first highly criticised, but was gradually accepted and finally became part of the aesthetic of the New Wave directors. Truffaut and Godard especially have made great use of the commentary and the interview technique where the image is more in the function of the words. Godard even goes farther and frequently adds titles in his effort to make the spectator as conscious of words as he is of things.

Except for one brief scene in the torture chamber, the scene of the abjuration and the

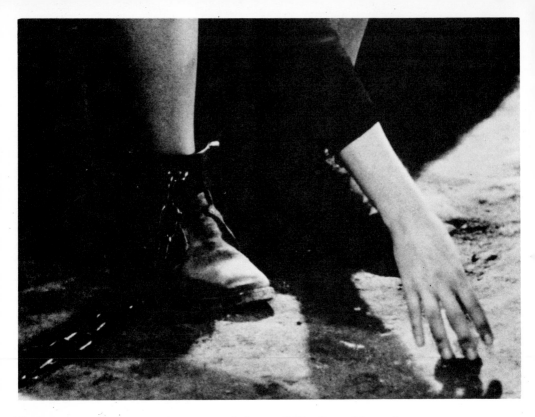

Still: Joan picks up the stone.

final sequence of the execution, most of the film takes place in the trial room and in Joan's cell. We witness a series of nine interrogations, five of them public in the trial room and four private in the cell. The private sessions were apparently illegal and at one point we see certain of the prelates walk out of the trial in protest against the Bishop's action which clearly exceeded his authority. Separating the interrogations and in counterpoint to them are scenes of Joan alone in her cell, of Joan and the soldiers or the monks walking up or down the tower stairway, of Cauchon and Warwick

discussing the trial or spying on Joan through a hole in the wall of her cell, of Joan with Brother Isambart, her counsellor, and another monk who come to advise and help her. Finally, after all the interrogations, there is the public abjuration in the market place, followed by a scene in her cell when she retracts the abjuration, then her preparation for death, reception of Holy Communion and the execution.

The counterpoint in these scenes is established not simply by a change of place which would not necessarily add a great deal by way of contrast, but by a corresponding change of technique. During the interrogations the camera is always fixed and the point of view is changed by a change of shot. In the other scenes the shots are longer and the camera moves more freely, following people in corridors or on the stairway, moving down to Joan's feet or the feet of the soldiers and monks. In her cell, the camera sometimes tilts down to Joan's chains, and once, in a typically Bressonian movement, it follows Joan's hand as she stoops to pick up a stone that someone has thrown through her cell window, then tilts up again as she rises.

In all of these scenes time and space are fragmented, as they generally are in Bresson's films, according to their perception by the main character. We never get a complete view of the trial room or of the cell or the market place, but only the objects or people that interest Joan at any particular instant. In her cell her eyes are generally cast down and she never looks around the entire room. Neither does the camera. When her attention is called to certain objects, the stairway, the door, the stone, the window, her chains, the hole in the wall, then we see these things, too, but no more. In the trial room the camera photographs only the person speaking. The presence of others is more felt than seen. Their faces, when we do catch sight of them behind Joan when she is speaking, are more like masks than human countenances. They become almost decorative elements, a harmonious distribution of blacks, whites, and greys, the colours of the monks' robes and of the soldiers' uniforms. There is a certain dialectic in this presentation of space, which is constantly oscillating between the concrete and the abstract. Concretely the images contain bodies, material objects, full of weight and density, but on the other hand, we never see more than a part of this reality, bits and chunks of which are separated from the rest, as they

must be in the cinema. Bresson deliberately turns what might seem a limitation of the medium to his advantage by insisting upon it, by reducing the field of vision of the camera, and consequently of the spectator, to the field of Joan's vision. Two or three times in the film this perspective is changed and becomes that of others who are watching Joan, notably of Cauchon and Warwick as they spy on her through the hole in the wall of her cell. Here the narrow vision of the prosecutors is emphasised by placing the camera on their side of the wall and shooting through the hole. The resulting image gives us a tiny picture of Joan framed by the irregular edge of the hole, and the rest of the screen is black.

Except for the opening scene, the petition for rehabilitation which took place twenty-five years after Joan's death, the film follows the events of the trial and execution chronologically as they are recorded in the minutes between 21st February, 1431 and 30th May, 1431. The time may be chronological, but it would be impossible to call it historical. No dates are mentioned, there are no concrete references to the historical situation except in the presence of the English in a part of France that was in fact 'occupied' at the time. We hear nothing of the political motivation behind Joan's trial, although in an introductory text following the titles at the beginning of the film, Bresson had written, 'The interests at stake are known.' The film records Joan's trial for witchcraft. We are not told who is king nor who is pope but we do know that there is a council being held at Basle. Joan's advisors urge her to appeal to the pope and the council, which she does, but the appeal is refused by Cauchon, another act that exceeded his authority. 'The replies of Joan to the questions that are put to her, serve not so much to give us information about events present or past (delivery of Orléans, coronation of the king, her capture) as to provoke upon her face in the film, the significant movements of her soul.' (Robert Bresson in *Amor-Film*, Lyon.)

Despite the alternation of night and day in the film, the element of time is not important. Time is fragmented as it would be in prison life and as it was in *A Man Escaped* and in *Pickpocket*. The dearth of historical allusion as well as the way in which time is fragmented suggest that time is interior or it is presented, as is space, in the way that Joan perceives it. On one level this is true just as the rapidity of the rhythm (which is part of the time element) corresponds to the struggle that is going on in her soul. It is curious to notice how, as the English become more impatient and anxious to get the trial over with, the rhythm of the film tends to slow down until the moment when Joan herself is worn down and gives in. When she makes her abjuration, her time, the time of the film and real time, that of the prosecutors, coincide, but only for an instant because after she retracts her abjuration the rhythm of the film speeds up again hastening on to its inevitable conclusion, her death.

This feeling of inevitability pervades the film from the start. Everyone knows the story of Joan of Arc, so there can be no real suspense. The film begins with the petition for rehabilitation which took place twenty-five years after Joan's death. The drum-roll creates an atmosphere of tension and reminds us of an execution. The interrogations themselves are conducted swiftly. The English are constantly telling Bishop Cauchon to hurry up and cut the trial short. After the second interrogation Warwick says in English, 'Don't forget, she must be burned,' and the statement is repeated in French by one of the judges. In the last sequence the camera follows Joan's bare feet as she runs to the stake. Throughout the film there are recurrent shots of Joan's feet in her heavy shoes and chains which make it difficult for her to walk, but at the end, freed from the shoes

and chains, she actually runs to her death.

The actuality of Joan's story results also from Bresson's deliberate avoidance of anything like an historical style. 'I hope to have made the marvellous girl *actual*. It is the privilege of the cinematographer to put the past in the present provided he avoids the historical style like the plague.' (Bresson in *Etudes Cinématographiques*.) The lack of attention to historical detail, the costumes of an undefined period (the robes of the prelates and monks are the same as those worn today): all of this leaves us free to hear Joan's words in much the same way as she heard her voices and realise their significance for today. They are not fixed in another age, but have a meaning that is timeless. Bresson was right to attach so great an importance to Joan's words and to construct his film around them.

From one point of view at least the film itself is an act of faith. 'I see her with the eyes of a believer. I believe in the mysterious world upon which she opens a door and closes it.' (Bresson in an interview with André Parinau in *Arts*.) And one of the things that struck Bresson most about the story of Joan was the analogy of her passion with that of Christ: betrayed to the enemy for a price, she is abandoned by her friends, tried illegally on false charges, tortured and finally put to death. This happened because of her fidelity to a vocation that she firmly believed came to her from God. On one level the film is the representation of Joan's trial. On another it is a description of the mysterious ways in which God's grace is at work in a world that has been tainted by sin.

This second element appears first of all in the dialogue to which Bresson deliberately gave so important a place. He carefully selected questions and answers that showed the strength of the girl and her confidence in the authenticity of her vocation as well as her simple yet profound faith. The first interrogation is a series of statements about what she is bound to answer under oath. Her final reply is as follows: 'I will say what I know, but not everything. I have come from God and have only to do his will here and I ask only to be sent back to God from whom I came.'

The second interrogation is about her voices which are for her the sign of God's care and

Still: Joan spied on by her captors.

the proof of her mission. She boldly replies to the Bishop, 'Be careful of what you are doing, for, in truth, I am sent on the part of God and you place yourself in great danger.' She declares she is ready for anything that will please God and that without his grace she could do nothing. It is at this point that the well-known question is asked, 'Do you believe you are in the grace of God?' To which she answers, 'If I am not, may God put me there; if I am, may God keep

Still: Warwick.

me there.' The answer is emphasised by having Cauchon look at the secretaries and then by a cut to their hands as they record the question and by the sound of the quills scratching on the paper. This emphasis was hardly necessary and seems a fault in the film that was so deliberately stripped down to the essential. Joan's answer stands on its own. The technique however does add a bit of variety to the monotony of the interrogation. It also indicates something of Bresson's attitude and is perhaps more interesting from that point of view than for what it adds to the film.

The other interrogations continue in the same way with Joan constantly reiterating her faith and confidence and the judges trying to undermine that faith, to sow doubt or to trap her in some statement that will convict her of witchcraft. Her answers are always intelligent and lucid as she evades their traps every time. She continues to affirm that her mission is from God. 'With all my power I accomplished the commandment of God, dictated by my voices and according to my own understanding of them.' At the end of the admonition the Bishop asks once more if she is willing to submit to the Church. She replies, 'What is the Church? I will not submit myself to you or to your judgment. You are my capital enemy.' Finally just before the abjuration when the prosecutors are doing their best to wear her down, she says defiantly, 'I have done nothing wrong. I believe in the twelve articles of the faith and the ten commandments of the Decalogue. I refer myself to the Council and to the Pope of Rome. And I wish to believe everything the Holy Church believes.'

Beyond this dialogue which makes obvious statements about faith, hope and the grace of God, there are certain elements of Bresson's style, which, combined with the dialogue, reinforce the religious meaning of the film. The rhythm despite the realism of certain elements (countenances, material objects, sounds, etc.), prevents the film from belonging to a genre that could be called realistic. The dialectic of the concrete and the abstract as well as the representation of time and space as perceived by Joan are further elements in what Susan Sontag has called Bresson's 'spiritual style'.

Reality is presented in such a way as to force us to understand that what we see and hear is not its sum total. This seems all the more true when we consider Bresson's use of the ellipsis in the film. The ellipsis is a common enough rhetorical device and has been used in the cinema almost from the start and frequently enough for exactly the same reasons that Bresson uses it. Although ellipsis is characteristic of his style, it appears more constantly and perhaps more effectively in *The Trial of Joan of Arc* than in any of his previous films.

In the opening scene the camera never shows us Joan's mother's face. The first interrogation begins with a shot of Joan's bound hands on the book of the Gospels. Scenes begin in the middle of an interrogation or of a reply by Joan and

sometimes end with questions unanswered. Meaning is conveyed by looks and by gestures as often as by words. There is in the shooting script of the film a long speech by Brother Isambart, Joan's counsellor, instructing her on the manner in which she should reply to the inquisitors. While making the film, Bresson decided to substitute a simple gesture for this speech, yet none of the meaning is lost. The presence of the soldiers or monks is frequently conveyed by shots of their feet. A single voice, rather disconcertingly effeminate, shouting, 'Burn the witch'! in English, represents the crowd. When Cauchon asks Joan to recite the *Pater*, she says, 'Hear my Confession. I'll say it in Confession.' Cauchon ignores the request and goes on with the interrogation, and the implication is that he is less at home in the sacramental tribunal than in this false tribunal. The scene in which Joan's virginity is verified is admirable from this point of view of ellipsis and suggestion. We see three women whose backs are turned to the camera move slowly towards it and out of the frame. Joan is sitting on her bed with the sheet over her. The camera moves closer to her as she pulls the sheet up over her face until only her eyes can be seen, a gesture at once of modesty and of defiance as she looks towards the wall of her cell. This corresponds beautifully to the first mention of Joan's virginity while Cauchon and Warwick had been spying on her through the hole in the wall.

There are several sequences of an extreme simplicity yet enormously complex in all that they imply. Just one example: the sequence is composed of six different scenes, all but one extremely brief:

1) Outside the trial room: Warwick with a young Englishman stops the Bishop and says, 'If it's her virginity that gives her strength, we'll make her lose her virginity.'

2) Cut to the tower: Warwick and the English-

man enter and send the guards away. They descend the stairway and look into Joan's room as they pass the open door.

3) Cut to Joan's room: she sits with her back to the door not suspecting that she is being watched. An eye appears at the hole in the wall and we hear the Englishman say, in English, 'I'd thrash her with pleasure, but her virginity . . . I'll never strip her of those clothes which protect her. No one in the world could.' Warwick replies, 'The bishop and his churchmen could.'

4) Cut to the tower: A woman enters carrying a dress. She descends the stairway.

5) Joan's room: The dress is put on her bed. Joan picks it up and looks at it. The bishop and several others are there. The bishop asks, 'What do you think of the dress that is offered to you?' She answers, putting the dress back on the bed, 'As long as it pleases our Lord, I will not take it. But if I must be led to condemnation, and I have to undress, I ask the favour of having a woman's shift and something on my head. I prefer to die rather than revoke what our Lord has had me do, and I believe firmly that he will not permit me to fall so low without coming to my help even by a miracle.'
Bishop: Since you wear man's clothing by the will of God, why do you ask for a woman's shift in case of death?
Joan: It is enough for me that it be long.
Bishop: Several times, and especially yesterday, you asked us to hear Mass because of the solemnity of the holy days.
Joan: I ask to be allowed to hear Mass and to receive Communion on the feast of Easter.
Bishop: Joan, put aside man's clothing and we will grant you this favour. (The bishop and the others leave.)
Cut to the hole in the wall where we see the eye of the Englishman, then cut back to Joan, who, alone, says, 'I will not hear Mass and I will not receive Communion on the feast of Easter.'

6) As the previous image fades, we hear Church bells ringing. The new image fades in, the bells are still ringing. Joan is sitting on her bed. Brother Isambart stands before her. They listen motionless. Joan wipes away her tears. She says, 'Those who were on my side, what are they doing? Have they forgotten me?' Brother Isambart leaves; the bells ring more loudly. The image fades.

The relations set up in this sequence are extraordinarily complex and subtle. The sequence begins by linking Joan's *spiritual* strength with her virginity. Then the young Englishman connects her virginity with the clothes she wears. There is a hint of voyeurism as the two men watch Joan through the hole in the wall and a hint of sadism in their conversation. A certain complicity between Warwick and Cauchon is evident from Warwick's statement that the Churchmen could strip Joan of her man's clothing especially since this statement is followed immediately by the scene with the dress which is offered to Joan by Cauchon.

Earlier in the film she said that her voices had told her that God wanted her to remain a virgin. She says now that she could not fall so low, that is, refuse to obey God, without his coming to her aid even by a miracle if necessary – and yet, she asks for a woman's shift if they put her to death. When Cauchon asks her why, since this seems to contradict what she had already said, she does not answer. And in this simple refusal to respond lies a world of meaning. Joan has also made the connection between her man's clothing and her virginity. But at the moment of her death she can surrender without fear, and put on a woman's dress, because in dying she gives herself entirely, body and soul, to God. The woman's dress then becomes almost a wedding garment, a sign of her surrender.

When Joan refuses to answer his question, Cauchon changes the subject and tries to bribe her by offering Holy Communion on Easter Sunday in exchange for her accepting woman's clothing. The camera cuts to the hole in the wall where the Englishman is watching, perhaps anticipating Joan's reaction, but at any rate extremely interested in how she will reply. The matter is settled when she says she will neither hear Mass nor receive communion on Easter. As the image fades we hear Church bells ringing. It is obviously Easter Sunday. Joan in her cell with Brother Isambart is weeping. She is still wearing her man's clothing and she has not received communion. At that moment a great wave of loneliness sweeps over her and she asks if those who had been on her side have forgotten her. Brother Isambart goes out leaving Joan alone as the bells ring even more loudly than before. There is an obvious connection between Joan's suffering and the mystery of Easter Sunday which celebrates the victory of Christ over death. This is an anticipation of the final scene where Joan's deliverance by fire will also be her victory over her persecutors.

Joan is finally allowed to receive Holy Communion just before her execution. Brother Isambart says as he gives her the host, 'Do you believe that this is the body of Christ?' She answers, 'Yes, and the only one that can deliver me.' Then the executioner enters with the long gown. Joan raises her hands over her head to receive the gown, but this is also a gesture of surrender. Here we have the dress as a wedding gown and sign of her surrender to God. She says to Brother Isambart, 'Where shall I be tonight?' He asks, 'Don't you have hope in the Lord?' She answers, 'Yes, and with God's help, I shall be in Paradise.' Her chains are removed and as she leaves the cell the camera dwells on the empty chain.

In the market place, after a final admonition by the bishop, Joan asks for the cross. One of the monks goes to get it but in the meantime a soldier makes one out of two sticks and gives it to her. As she runs to the stake, the camera frames on her bare feet. The image corresponds to the opening shot of the film where we had seen her Mother's feet walking slowly and laboriously down the aisle of the cathedral and to other shots of feet; Joan's in her large shoes and chains, the soldiers' in their heavy boots, the monks' in their sandals. She has a rosary in her hand and as she runs the tiny cross precedes her all the way to the steps of the scaffold where she drops it. The camera focuses on the steps just before she mounts them. Throughout the film there had been a recurring image of the tower stairway that led from the trial room to Joan's cell. This is the last time she will climb a stairway since now she is mounting to her death – but also to life. As Joan turns the bright sunlight strikes her full in the face. It is the only time in the film Bresson permits himself any kind of heavy contrast in the lighting. At the stake she is tied by the executioner and his assistant. The camera follows the movement of the rope that binds her, starting from a low position and rising and coming to rest upon her face. The fire is lighted and catches quickly. The crowd, which we hardly see at all, but which has been shouting, becomes silent. A church-bell rings in the distance. The crackling of the flames grows louder. Smoke envelopes the scaffold. The monk arrives with the processional cross from a nearby church and holds it up before Joan. When she sees it she cries out in a loud voice, 'The voices that I had were from God. All that I did, I did by the commandment of God. No, my voices did not deceive me. The revelations that I had were from God.' When we first saw her at the beginning of the film, her bound hands were spread on the book of the Gospels as she swore to tell the truth. Now, before the crucifix, as she is dying, she affirms the truth of all she had said and done. (As the noise of the flames becomes unbearable we see the chains fall off, eaten through by the heat, an image that

Still: Joan is bound to the stake.

contrasts with that of her bound hands at the beginning of the film.) All the prelates sitting on the tribunal suddenly rise as one man and stand fixedly watching the scaffold. Joan is now completely hidden by the smoke and flame. We hear her cry 'Jesus!'. The camera shows us the prelates still fixed as though unable to move, but the two monks with the cross are forced to move back from the flame. There is an image of a dog wandering through the crowd. Some pigeons can be seen on the roof of the tribunal where the churchmen still stand motionless. As the smoke and flames die down we see the charred remains of the stake and chain, empty now. Joan has disappeared. The camera dwells on the empty stake. We hear the same drum-roll as at the beginning and the film is ended.

Bresson refuses symbolic meanings for the dog and the pigeons. They simply represent life which must go on even though the spectators stand fixed. The movement and sound of the birds' wings corresponds to the movement and sound of the flames. But because of this and Bresson's insistence on the idea of life, there may also be some deeper meaning here. Joan's death is really for her the beginning of a new life, one for which she had longed and in which she had expressed confidence. This is fairly clear from the images: her bare feet running to the scaffold, the insistence on the ladder that Joan must climb, the rising movement of the camera, the chains falling away to signify a release, and finally the bare stake pointing to the sky. The life of the animals also signifies Joan's new life, the life of grace. The spectators, particularly the English officers and the prelates who were responsible for Joan's death, are fixed, immovable, obstinate in their refusal to accept that same life. That it was Bresson's intention to make the supernatural appear through the circumstances and events of Joan's life is also evident from what he has said about his film. 'It seems to me that the emotion here, in this trial (and in this film), should come not so much from the agony and death of Joan as from the strange air that we breathe while she talks of her Voices, or of the crown or of the angel, just as she would talk of one of us or of this glass or of this carafe. What St. Ignatius would demand a century later, this familiarity with a palpable supernatural, Joan's genius reached without the shade of a difficulty.' (Interview in *Etudes Cinématographiques*.)

In *The Trial of Joan of Arc*, Robert Bresson seems to be at the extreme limit of his quite considerable talent. It was a fantastic risk to try to portary this 'familiarity with a palpable supernatural.' To some, the attempt might seem doomed to failure from the start since what he wants to do is show what is spiritual by means that are material; in a sense, to portray transcendence through incarnation. From a theological point of view, there is a striking analogy here with what happened when the Son of God became man. And even the person of Jesus of Nazareth was apparently not lacking the same ambiguity that is certainly present in Bresson's film. Some few people recognised him as the Son of God; the vast majority did not. Whether or not one sees *The Trial of Joan of Arc* as a film about the experience of God's grace depends to a large extent on one's beliefs. The characters of the film, including Joan, are ambiguous. As Bresson said, 'I have tried to make Joan as possible and true to life – or as impossible and as untrue to life – as she was then.' In Dreyer's *Passion of Joan of Arc*, the forces of good are quite clearly distinguished from the forces of evil by the contrast of light and shadow, in the composition of the images, in the costumes – it is astonishing to see how even the folds of a monk's habit can become sinister – and above all in the countenances and acting of his interpreters. Bresson permits himself little or no contrast in the lighting, except at the very end. It is generally uniform and neutral, and the predominant colour of the film is grey. Except for the chains and the stake, and possibly also Joan's shoes, the décor, the properties and costumes are purely functional and not symbolic. The expression on Joan's face as she answers the questions hardly differs from that of Cauchon as he asks them.

And yet we are aware of subtle differences. We perceive distinctions between good and evil even though Bresson refrains from emphasizing them. These differences come through, not in the expression, but in the timbre, the colour of the voices of Florence Delay as Joan and of Jean-Claude Fourneau as Cauchon, and Bresson has acknowledged his debt to the non-professional performers.

The distinctions also come through in the way he uses his camera. In the interrogations Cauchon is always photographed straight on without any variation in the camera angle. Joan is photographed from different angles. This, I feel, is an anticipation of the final scene of Joan's death where the Bishop and prelates are fixed in their inflexibility, while Joan sometimes hesitates; she is more flexible, perhaps at moments she is tempted to doubt the authenticity of her voices and vision – this is what Cauchon is trying to make her do – or she is docile, turning to Brother Isambart for counsel. Sometimes the camera watches as she listens to Cauchon's questions, her eyes downcast, her head tilted slightly forward, and it continues to watch as, in the same shot, she answers, her head raised slightly, her eyes open and looking at Cauchon. This slight movement is enough to give physical expression to the interior resistance of the girl just as the change of camera angle mentioned above shows her struggle with herself, but also her docility – docility not only to her earthly counsellor but also to her voices and to what they represent, the will of God.

'One would say that she was a more perfect being than we are, more sensitive. She combines her five senses in a new way. She *sees* her *voices*. She convinces us of a world at the limit of our faculties. She penetrates into this supernatural world but she closes the door behind her.' (Bresson in *Etudes Cinématographiques*, emphasis mine.) Perhaps by combining images and dialogue in the unusual way that he does in this film, Bresson is also trying to make us see the voices. At any rate the Joan that he describes in the statement just cited is the one he attempted to portray, a woman at once sensitive and a mystic, whose voices indeed came from another world to which she alone seemed to have entry. He may have been trying to suggest this idea by the repeated shots of doors opening and closing. And yet if my own reading of Bresson's film is correct, he is also saying that those who are not fixed, hardened to the grace of God, may perhaps also have access to this same world. While the prelates and soldiers stand motionless, their faces totally inexpressive, the two monks who had sympathised with Joan and tried to help her, suffer with her as they hold the crucifix and are forced to move by the heat of the fire.

Here again lies all the significance of Bresson's deliberate ambiguity. First of all the film is open to many interpretations. One can see it as a tribute to resistance against the enemy in an occupied country, a theme already seen in *A Man Escaped*. Or it can be seen as the '...trial of the just man's stifled liberty, a particularly modern and "existential" theme, as well as the trial of the witness of sanctity.' (Jean d'Yvoire in *Télérama*.) Or it can be seen as an indictment of the world not only of Joan's time but of all time, which is not yet ready, in Shaw's words, to receive its saints or those who have the courage to listen to the voices. The film could also be seen as an indictment of the Church which has so often been willing to compromise with secular authorities in order to protect its own material interests and has repeatedly silenced, excommunicated or burned its prophets and reformers when they have tried to recall it to its proper mission. Finally, it can be seen as what the present analysis makes it out to be, a story of how '...it pleased God to act through the intermediary of a simple girl,' and that girl's will to be faithful.

'When they asked her, "how did you know that it was Saint Michael?" she answered, "Because he had an angel's voice." "How do you know that it was an angel's voice?" "Because I had the will to believe it." Will which was added to the apparition. She had need of her will to reach the kingdom.' (Bresson in *Etudes Cinématographiques*.) As Bresson presents the matter in his film, it was not sufficient for the grace of God, that is, the apparition, to be given to Joan. She could not have entered the Kingdom if her own will had not been added to the grace of God.

As we have seen, Bresson has said that his film was entirely in questions and answers. But this question and answer technique is not limited to the dialogue or to the interrogation scenes. At one point Joan gives an answer, is not sure that it is correct and looks to Brother Isambart for counsel. He simply nods his head. Her look was the question, his nod the answer. After Joan retracts her abjuration, Cauchon meets Warwick on the stairway and simply looks at him. The bishop says, 'We have her. She is caught.' Warwick's look is a question, the Bishop's statement the answer. In the scene when Cauchon tries to make Joan give up her man's clothing, the cut to the hole in the wall is a question, Joan's statement, 'I will not hear Mass nor receive Communion on Easter,' the answer. This dialectic of question and answer continues right to the very end. The empty scaffold poses the most fundamental question about Joan's faith, perhaps about faith in general, and for those who believe, it also contains the answer to that question. In this same final image, the full force of the film's ambiguity is most strongly felt. Some will see here nothing more than an empty scaffold, a charred and smoking stake pointing obscenely toward the sky, a vulgar symbol of despair. Others, who, like Bresson, have grasped the analogy of Joan's Passion with that of Christ, will see the stake as the upright of the cross, which, by the marvellous paradox of Christianity, symbolises not despair but hope, not punishment but reward, not death but life.

Finally, we may say with Jean d'Yvoire, 'Between sanctity and pride, between heaven and hell, there is the ambiguity of man. Perhaps this gives the intimate key to Bresson's entire poetic style.'

Still: The last shot of The Trial of Joan of Arc.

AU HASARD, BALTHAZAR

CHARLES BARR

Half-way through *Balthazar* we see the tramp figure, Arnold, giving donkey-rides to tourists in the hills. He has two donkeys, one of them Balthazar himself. Two tourists discuss painting, another pair the psychology of the criminal. Both conversations are significant, providing insight into the methods and themes of the film.

A typical start, this, to the kind of exposition of a film that wraps it up neatly, too neatly. All criticism involves distortion, but with Bresson the danger is especially great because of the difficulty of rendering on paper the 'feel' of his films, the most important thing about them. Writing after several viewings or with a script in hand, it's easy to short-cut the actual experience of watching the screen and following a narrative in time. Even if one thinks more highly of *Balthazar* than John Coleman does, it must be admitted that his description of it as 'almost comic in its witholding of information' gives a more accurate account of what it's like to experience than do most pro-Bresson articles. Who, at first viewing, understands all he feels he ought to about the father's lawsuit, the suspected murder, Gérard's employment? And Bresson's detailed *mise-en-scène* is as cryptic (an apt word, with its root meaning of 'concealing') as his narrative. The donkey-ride sequence is like *The Trial of Joan of Arc* in its visual austerity. Though Arnold's presence is significant, we see him only at the very end, in a reaction shot as he takes in what the last speaker has said. Earlier, Bresson has let us glimpse a pair of sandalled feet going briefly past the camera, so we know the donkeys are

being led and can infer it's by Arnold, but this is all (the first sentence of this article is, strictly, inaccurate). There are separate shots of the donkeys' feet and – in formal succession – of the four riders during their conversations. At the end Arnold is framed alone, not linked with them in the same shot. As in *Joan of Arc*, the need to work out who is where and take on trust the spatial relationship between the various elements in a scene may be found distracting, even alienating (see Ian Cameron's comments on the earlier film in *Movie 7*). It can be argued that the cryptic method, in *Balthazar* if not *Joan of Arc*, justifies itself, and that the film could not be other than it is. Either way, to 'flatten out' the style intellectually is to lose the film. You could say that Bresson states this obliquely in the first of the conversations I've referred to. An artist tells his companion about his approach to painting. He explains at some length how he depicts not the waterfall itself but 'what it tells him'. His friend therefore suggests '*Une peinture cérébrale? Une peinture de pensée?*' No: '*Une peinture d'action.* Action-painting.'

In terms of cinema Bresson of all directors doesn't limit himself to recording external reality in a passive way, he imposes his own vision of it, but this doesn't make his work into cerebral cinema, filmed thought that can be translated back painlessly from image into concept, from story and dialogue into ideas. (Of course one can't avoid doing this all the time, but this only underlines the limitations of film criticism.) Even Bresson's cinema, or

Still: Balthazar and his tormentors.

perhaps especially Bresson's cinema, is action-cinema, in both the term's possible meanings.

Bresson moves straight on to the next pair's talk about guilt. The first man wonders: can one be held responsible for a crime that one commits without willing it, and without any memory of it, in a state when (because of, say, drugs or alcohol) 'the conscious mind gives place to the subconscious?' His companion develops this: '...or even to the unconscious, in such a way that no trace remains, and the criminal isn't aware of being a criminal?'

After these words comes the reaction shot of Arnold, looking back as he's struck by what they say. Then a brief scene of Arnold under the night sky, waking from a dream and swearing solemnly never to drink again. Cut to a bar counter: Arnold gets drunk. He goes on to

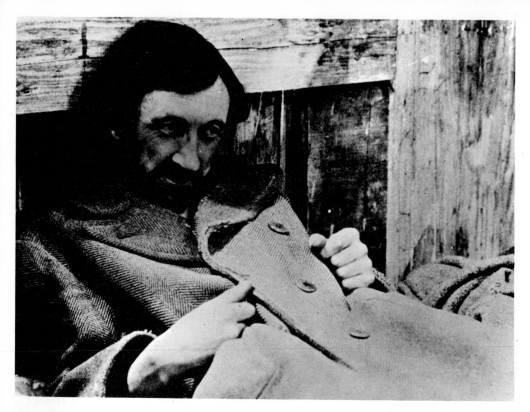

attack Balthazar savagely, and thus lose him, for he runs away. It's a clear enough illustration of the riders' problem. Is Arnold guilty? He didn't know what he was doing when he beat Balthazar, but we naturally ask also: was he not responsible for breaking his oath and getting drunk in the first place? The way Bresson shoots the bar scene is significant. Arnold's voice asks for a drink, his hand lifts the glass and puts it down empty, it's filled again, his hand lifts it and puts it down empty again and he sprawls drunkenly across the counter. This is in one brief shot without camera movement:

when he drinks he lifts the glass out of frame left. Thus we are shown the *act* in isolation, its isolation in the frame indicating its independence of Arnold's conscious will. It's significant too that there's been no intermediate scene showing the weakening of Arnold's resolve; indeed we don't know how long a time has elapsed. One shot simply follows another. We don't see his will broken down, we see will and action working independently. Bresson's setting-out of this episode suggests that Arnold is no more or less 'responsible' for getting drunk than he is for his drunken actions.

As a character says in Iris Murdoch's *The Unicorn*, 'There are acts which belong to people somehow regardless of their wills.' And not only to Arnold.

How guilty then is he? Balthazar 'forgives' him: when months later, by chance or design, Arnold visits the circus, Balthazar at once leaves off his act and rejoins him.

When Arnold returns home he's visited by the police. Persuaded that they have come to arrest him, he tries to shoot them; but the gun

Stills: Arnold. Below – with Gérard (left).

(unknown to him) is unloaded. Instead, they give him news of a legacy, and we cut straight to the celebration. Which might appear to reverse the logic of the earlier episode: Arnold has willed a crime but been unable to act it. One might expect him to be punished for his unacted intention as he was forgiven his 'unintended' acts. The contradiction can be resolved two ways: 1) he *is* punished. He gets no joy from the legacy, and he dies the same night. 2) He was not truly guilty. We saw Gérard lying to him about the policemen, and pressing the gun on him. Rather than willing

a crime he was submitting fatalistically to the will of another (of a practical joker: Gérard hadn't loaded the gun. Gérard is a tormentor, a devil).

Both points, I think, are valid together. Arnold is guilty, and punished; he is also innocent, and redeemed.

He receives a 'Judas kiss' before dying, from Gérard; he rides on an ass; he even, as Godard put it to Bresson in a *Cahiers* interview, has 'a little of the look of Christ'. Bresson replied 'Yes, but I did not seek that'. The association is there, but delicate: Arnold isn't a Christ figure, but you could say that the sins he takes upon him and dies for are the sins of all men. He is Everyman. The idea is enforced by Arnold's own story and by the context in which Bresson sets him. His weakness can't just be labelled alcoholism; Bresson uses it to stand for a more general human compulsion to submit to destructive forces.

Marie submits to Gérard. Their first contact is at night when Gérard and his friends creep into the grounds of the house and watch Marie alone with Balthazar, garlanding and kissing him. Marie then sits. She seems to hear the slight noise of Gérard's approach behind her. She lays her left hand beside her, on the bench.

Bresson frames her hand, alone; another hand, Gérard's, enters the frame and touches it. Marie runs away.

This comes long before the donkey-ride sequence but one naturally, in retrospect, applies the terms of the discussion to it. It is Marie's subconscious which has 'invited' Gérard, and with her conscious mind she disowns the act, as Arnold did his beating of Balthazar; but as with Arnold, Bresson pushes the analysis further, going on to show Marie 'choosing' Gérard as Arnold had chosen to drink. Again the *mise-en-scène* is everything. In their first love scene in the car, Bresson isolates their hands as though they had independent life. Close-ups of limbs are common enough in films good and bad, but the effect of Bresson's method is unique. While Gérard's hands are agents of his will, there's an overpowering sense of conflict between Marie's conscious will and the way she finds herself acting.

The effect, for all the precision with which Bresson creates it, is profoundly ambivalent. We see a character (Arnold, Marie) determining to act one way; we see the hand, and the body, acting decisively the other way. Are we to say: her actions show what Marie 'really' wants, what she *is* (the hypnotic concentration on the hand underlining, with a sort of irony, that this act is what counts)? Or: that the action takes place only on the physical plane (the isolation of the hand emphasising that it is 'only' a physical act and thus suggesting that the real self, the soul, can remain pure)?

In the short term, apparently the former, since the act is stronger than the will. Marie becomes committed to Gérard, and Arnold remains an alcoholic: they accept their states. Yet the very resignation with which they ultimately do so leaves open the possibility that

Still: Au hasard, Balthazar – *the first contact between Marie and Gérard.*

Still: Au hasard, Balthazar – *Gérard and his gang by the roadside.*

these states are unimportant. There is a strong feeling of predestination, almost Calvinism, about *Balthazar*. We can recognise a nobility, a grace, in Marie and Arnold which stays with them whatever they do. In contrast is Gérard. His first appearance (like theirs) colours everything he does thereafter. We see him with his gang, putting down oil on the road. They move off; eventually, a car passes them. Bresson cuts to a reverse shot of the car skidding off the road, then back to Gérard's satisfied reaction. Another car passes in the foreground and this time the noise of its crash is heard without cutting away from Gérard. The effect is extraordinary not just for its 'economy' of direction but for what it conveys about Gérard and his full, active responsibility for what he does. What he does to the car predicts what he will do to Marie's life. The crash is not something which happens 'outside' him and might thus in the last analysis or judgment be held not to belong to him. The oil and his clothes are black. He *is* what he does.

Marie by contrast is passive: things happen to her, as to Balthazar. Another profound ambivalence in the film is this: to juxtapose different things can suggest, broadly, comparison or contrast. Marie's life and Balthazar's progress along similar lines. He is present at many important moments for her. At the end she leaves home (dies?) and Balthazar dies on a hillside. What do these parallels convey? There is no trace of the classic, crude technique of animal-simile exploited by so many directors. The film's pattern can, conversely, be read as one of contrast, 'Marie descending, Balthazar ascending', yet it is hard to accept that this contains the whole truth either.

Clearly Balthazar is central to the film; he dominates it, and to have postponed him even till now is rather unnatural. In the film's first section, he is adopted by the children who spend their summers together. Bresson, by the marvellous delicacy with which he co-ordinates images and music, binds together images of sorrow and joy into a serene unity. When Jacques gets into the car to go home, and says goodbye, the reverse shot frames not the family but the baby donkey at their feet; the young Marie peeps out beside him. This, the final shot of the section, is Jacques's image. The very spareness of Bresson's style gives it this charge: it's not one shot among many, it's the only image we have to remember the moment by. (This is the film in microcosm; any further 'justification' of Bresson's cryptic method would be redundant.)

Years later Jacques returns. He and Marie talk about the dispute between their fathers. They look away and see Balthazar. Marie says 'Yes, it's Balthazar', and Jacques echoes her: 'Balthazar. Oh, Marie, everything is just as it used to be; and you are more beautiful than ever. You remember what I promised...' (their childhood pledge of love, made on the same bench where they're now sitting). While

Stills: Marie and Jacques; Marie's parents.

Jacques speaks, Bresson holds the camera steadily on Balthazar, almost as though it were Balthazar whom he were addressing, not Marie. In a way this is so, for he's thinking not so much of the Marie in front of him as of the memories 'triggered' by Balthazar, of their childhood. Jacques's image hasn't altered.

Marie embraces him awkwardly, but things don't really seem to be as they were. Not only are Marie's thoughts disturbed by Gérard, but Jacques proceeds to have a row with her father and drives straight off, ignoring her.

We next see him towards the end of the film. Marie has been living under Gérard's spell, and her father has suffered in the lawsuit against Jacques's father. She and Jacques again sit on the bench and their reunion seems like another return to a more innocent life. He wants to marry her. Marie says how often she has dreamed of someone like Jacques who would forgive her. '*Mais aussi quel réveil, à devenir folle.*' There's a long pause, to allow Jacques, if he can, to take the hint as to what this awakening was and what Marie's life has been like. 'Now you know everything.' 'We'll be poor but I'll work twice as hard': the shallow romanti-

cism of this response irritates her. She gets up, telling him how futile is his fixation on their old life together as children, with Balthazar. It was '*un monde imaginaire, pas la réalité. La réalité est autre chose*'. She returns once more to Gérard.

This summary makes sense of the scene but gives little idea of its true content because, as at their last meeting, Balthazar is present and is made the scene's focus. As though cued by the word '*folle*' and its donkey associations, Bresson cuts away to him. He holds for a long time this shot of Balthazar placidly cropping the grass, bringing in the Schubert piano music with beautiful effect. Marie's words 'Now you know everything' follow this image and thus refer to it, inescapably. Balthazar represents the 'reality' which Jacques shows himself incapable of grasping.

The figure of Balthazar has as profound and complex a significance as Nature does for Wordsworth (indeed the parallels between Wordsworth and Bresson, particularly in the light of his last two films, seem to me interesting in all sorts of ways). For Jacques in this scene he is an assurance that nothing has changed since childhood, for Marie – and us – the reverse. One could compare this with the

double response, youthful and mature, to the scene at Tintern Abbey. It is what you bring to Nature, essentially, which colours it for you. By its continuing presence, its passiveness, it can be a reminder of past feelings and actions, a sort of repository for them. Balthazar is like this, and like the old man of whom Wordsworth wrote that 'The villagers in him / Behold a record which together binds / Past deeds . . .'

For Marie and for us, Balthazar in this scene with Jacques calls to mind all the meetings between her and Gérard at which he's been present (the wonderful sequence, for instance, in which their continuing relationship is conveyed by the waiting image of Balthazar, as summer turns to autumn and then winter). He was also there when Marie, in return for a night's shelter, gave herself to the miser. As far as this goes, Balthazar might as well be inanimate, like the milestone and telegraph pole which Arnold addresses, because they are there, in his strange death scene. The real inspiration in Bresson's use of Balthazar is what he lets him convey himself, as a living presence. He doesn't only remind Marie of sex, he represents it. Standing there, eating grass, he movingly evokes natural, sensual appetite. Reduced to words, it may sound improbable, but like all profound symbolism this ultimately is irreducible: one must simply experience it. Note in any case how Marie goes straight off, from Jacques, to feed Balthazar in his stall – then, for the last time, to Gérard. Frequently she has fondled Balthazar like this, quite sensuously, as a 'preparation' for Gérard, just as he had tormented Balthazar as a rehearsal for his treatment of her.

It could be maintained that Balthazar's sensuality is innocent, Marie's corrupt. Again, this is the basic ambivalence in the film's structure: comparison or contrast? I think the point ultimately is the former, the *continuity* between natural appetite (Balthazar) and the distortions it may undergo in the world. Marie and Arnold will not be condemned for their 'sins', any more than Mouchette: they are spiritually innocent, as they show in their first, loving, contacts with Balthazar. Where Gérard torments him, Marie fondles him, and Arnold saves him from death.

What makes the end so moving is that the whole experience of the film is concentrated in Balthazar. Like Ulysses in Tennyson's poem, he is a part of all that he has met. He bears the name traditionally given to one of the Three Wise Men, and he carries gold and perfume (the contraband belonging to Gérard and his gang). He lies down to die on a hillside among a flock of sheep. A lamb is kept very prominent in the frame. Again, the Christian associations are delicately present. Worldly goods are an acceptable tribute. They are not rejected for being Gérard's property. Do we not infer this too of Marie? Can we not say that, just as Balthazar, the instrument of Gérard's smuggling, is innocent of it, so Marie and Arnold are innocent of their sinful acts and are, like Mouchette and Joan of Arc, redeemed? If this seems perverse, in view of the apparent moral descent of Marie, one can only appeal again to the 'texture' of the film: to the way in which, repeatedly, judgments are stated only to be, at once, belied in action. Bresson never gives such reversals any ironic stress; his style presents contradiction and paradox as perfectly natural phenomena, from the very start of the film. The first shot is of the baby donkey. Marie's cousins are heard asking '*Donne le nous*'; their father replies '*Impossible*'. In the second shot they are leading him home.

Still: Balthazar lies dying on the mountain-side among a flock of sheep.

MOUCHETTE

CHARLES BARR

Of all Bresson's films, *Mouchette* is surely the most accessible, the easiest to respond to. One could imagine people going eagerly to a film they knew was about Joan of Arc, or a donkey, or a country priest, and getting an unpleasant shock at the kind of film Bresson's turned out to be; those interested by the idea of a film about a friendless fourteen-year-old who finally drowns herself are not, in my experience, disappointed by *Mouchette*. Unhelpful though it is to award respect to the art film in proportion as it is esoteric, one might be suspicious of the relative ease with which Bresson communicates here: it sounds alien to his methods, and the subject has its dangers. But, remarkably, Bresson makes this unesoteric film without at all modifying his distinctive elliptical style and tells a moving story of an oppressed child in a hostile world not only without being sentimental but without leaving *any* opening for the easy sentimental response.

These are difficult reconciliations to achieve. Even Dickens's toughest books and his least sentimentalised child-heroines have notoriously been sentimentalised by his readers. Something similar happens, I can't help feeling, with *Diary of a Country Priest*, Bresson's previous adaptation from Bernanos.

Both these films are, like much Victorian literature, based on a dialectic between involvement with the world and withdrawal from it. Both end in death. Mouchette's is suicide; the priest dies of cancer, but – as Raymond Durgnat brings out in his essay – there's a strong undertone of suicide about this and other elements in the film. He's too pale and weak to survive in this world, or to *will* survival. The film ends on the long-held image of the cross, as Dufréty's account of the priest's death is read on the soundtrack. In a formal reversal of this, Monteverdi's *Magnificat* (the film's only non-naturalistic sound) accompanies the final image of *Mouchette*, that of the girl's body submerged in the water. Two 'withdrawals', apparently, each powerfully endorsed by Bresson, yet the tone and final impact of the two films are strikingly different, for all their similarities in structure.

The priest is called child-like by the Vicar of Torcy, and again by the Countess: both the films set an 'innocent' against a society that lives by corruption, compromise, connivance. These are the more chilling for being so unspectacular, shown as so deeply rooted in humanity. There's no romantic opposition of country against town, children against adults – both films are set in country villages and children are among the most callous of their inhabitants. The Count – owner of the large estate that dominates Ambricourt – warns the priest not to try anything too ambitious in the parish but reconcile himself to what is *utile*, *efficace*. The same on a personal level: the Countess doesn't object to her husband's furtive affair with Louise, the governess. As Chantal (their daughter) puts it to the priest: '*Mama le trouve très convenable, très pratique*'. Such attitudes are characteristic of the world the priest encounters.

Still: Mouchette in school.

In *Mouchette*, Louise has an equivalent and near-namesake in Louisa, the barmaid who's fought over by Arsène (the poacher) and Mathieu (the gamekeeper). This triangle relationship is itself sufficiently strange: equally strange is the reaction of Mme Mathieu, or rather her lack of one. Twice, we see her at home with her husband: they seem to have an arrangement which is, in the terms used in the earlier film, convenient and practical. She encourages him in his campaign against Arsène's

poaching, and the implication may be that this covers Arsène's 'poaching' of Louisa. Although she's with Mathieu at the cafe when he is taunted about Louisa, she doesn't show any jealous response, nor does he seem to expect her to. Nor, above all, does Bresson seem to expect *us* to expect her to: there's no stress at all on her presence there. It's like the early scene where Mouchette's father and brother bring apparently smuggled liquor, at night, to the village café. They go to the back of the van to carry it in; when a police car draws up, shining torches, they hold a cover over the crates and stand there. The policemen look at them, see clearly what's going on, then drive away. It's a kind of accepted ritual, and presented as such: neither their connivance (of which there are other hints in the film) nor Mme Mathieu's is lingered on, or talked of. You could see this as another reminder of the affinity between Bresson and Godard. The bland objectivity of the style makes us see such connivance as *normal* in this world, in exactly the same way that it presents paradox as normal in the world of *Balthazar*.

Diary of a Country Priest isn't quite the same: in it, these things are made explicit, the priest attacks and tries to change them. Indeed, character is altogether more fluidly presented. People change, or reveal new aspects of themselves, as they come in contact with the priest. To Mouchette, other people are more or less fixed points, and we necessarily see little more of them than she does. She doesn't have a dialogue with people (indeed, she speaks very little in the whole film), she confronts them and responds to the way they define themselves. This response is clear and vigorous: throwing mud at her classmates, turning away in scorn (twice) from the boy who exposes himself to her, leaving Arsène's hut, and at the end rounding verbally both on her father ('*Merde!*') and on the death-obsessed old woman who gives her the shroud ('*Vous me dégoûtez, sale vieille bête!*'). All these responses end the contact, and she goes her own way – eventually to drown herself.

All this could make the film sound blacker than *Diary of a Country Priest*, but it doesn't work that way. Part of the reason is in Mouchette herself. Her suicide, paradoxically,

Still: Mouchette and Arsène.

doesn't resolve the film's dialectic in favour of withdrawal from the world, from life, in the way that the priest's death and the final image of the cross are felt to resolve the earlier film. Dying for Mouchette isn't the culmination of a steady refining process, the absorption of the physical into the spiritual, but an intensely physical act. The final scene is an absolutely superb conception, precisely realised. The suicide seems unpremeditated. She comes to a

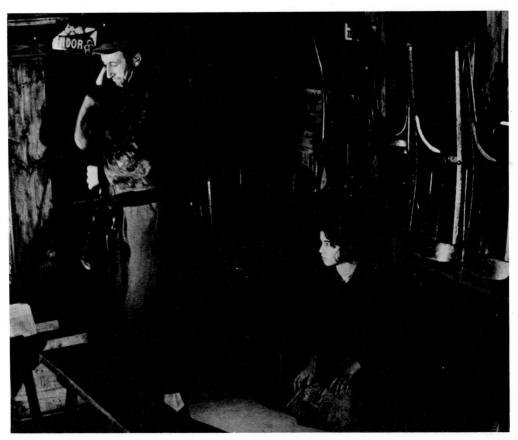

hillock with water at the bottom of it: her rolling down it is like a game, a way to wrap herself up in the dress given her by the old woman. One can't tell at what point she gets the idea of drowning, but insofar as it's a conscious choice, it is a circumstantial, almost capricious one, based on her immediate mood, her alienation from people at this moment. She accepts death not because she's weary of life but because others have *denied* her life: the shopkeeper deploring her sensuality, the old woman pressing her own obsession with the dead on her, and so on. We can't doubt that if

Stills: Mouchette.

the occasion for death hadn't presented itself – or if the tractor-driver to whom she waved before rolling down the second time had responded – she would have gone back, carrying the milk for her baby brother, profoundly alive, instinctive and resilient as she is. An essential part of the film's meaning is there, irreducibly, in her face, body and sensuous movements (compare the figures of the priest and Balthazar the donkey in their respective films): the way she grinds and pours coffee, throws the lid of

the pot dextrously back into place, caresses Arsène in his fit, sings to him, clasps him even as he rapes her, washes up glasses, warms the baby's milk against her breast, rolls downhill, rides a dodgem car at the fair.

This last, crucial episode has no equivalent in the novel, nor, as far as I know, is there anything like it in Bresson's work (though the comparison with the nearest thing to it in *Diary of a Country Priest*, the priest's brief, essentially wistful, pillion ride on a motor-cycle, is suggestive): the context is worth describing.

Sunday morning. Going to mass, Mouchette stamps rhythmically in a puddle, splashing mud. Her father chases her, catches her up by the Church door and gives her a violent push. She lands up against the font containing holy water. Dipping her finger in this, she makes the sign of the cross: fade out, then in on a shot of her washing glasses behind a bar. Fairground noise and music. The manager pays her some money, which she hands over to her father. He gives her a drink, then she drifts over towards the dodgems. A woman with a baby buys a token and gives it to Mouchette, who takes a free car; when they start, a young man keeps ramming her. She responds with growing exhilaration.

If, as I suggested, there's a dialectic in Bresson between involvement in the world and withdrawal from it, this section superbly dramatises the impulse to involvement and acceptance. It doesn't matter that she finds herself at the font by 'chance', she *accepts* the chance and crosses herself instantly, with no pause to get into a suitable unworldly mood. Then straight from holy water to dishwater as though to stress a continuity. For me, this evokes the hymn by George Herbert beginning 'Teach me, my God and King / In all things

Stills: Mouchette. *Bottom and opposite page – before and during the fairground sequence.*

Stills: Mouchette and Arsène.

thee to see'. . . 'Who sweeps a room, as for thy laws, / Makes that and the action fine.' (And in this, Mouchette recalls the woman in the important last scene of *Diary of a Country Priest*, the mistress of the priest's old colleague Dufréty). The gift of the token, when she has no money to buy one, is a mystery which she just accepts, unquestioning. At first viewing we imagine we may have failed to recognise some friend or relative of Mouchette's, but the woman is a complete stranger. The dodgem scene itself is moving and exhilarating on more than one level: it conveys the buffetings of the world which Mouchette can take and relish and 'push against' joyfully so long as there's some recognition of herself as an individual – as there is by the boy.

When the ride ends he walks over to a

shooting gallery, watching for her to follow; she does so, and is meeting his eyes in the start of a really beautiful smile when her father, with customary brutality, intervenes. Nothing is said, and the incident isn't referred to again, but it's impossible to forget it. The boy looks as though he's middle-class and comes from outside the village; Mouchette's tragedy is that, especially after her mother's death, those within her small orbit don't show a comparable awareness of her. It's as though she were being buffeted by riderless dodgems, with the music switched off. I don't think you can condemn her for her moment of despair, nor Bresson for constructing the society about her with too wilful a glumness. He makes that society wholly and chillingly believable yet doesn't insist that it's the full story of humanity. The memory of the fair remains vivid; there is also Mouchette herself, and the complex impact of her suicide.

Just as such a death in real life would force people to look back at their own behaviour with a new scrutiny, so this fictional death makes the audience look back over the film in a more intense and analytical way than if Mouchette had simply, as she could well have done, immersed · herself in life again. It fixes our revulsion against the life surrounding her, the way people have dealt with her. These *are* intolerable: after her death we can't, charitably blurring our impressions, feel (or imagine we are encouraged to feel) 'Life's like that, one has to face it'. Compare the uncomfortably upbeat ending of a film like Bergman and Sjöberg's *Frenzy*: the equivalent ending to *Mouchette*, however much more honest than *Frenzy*'s, would still have been hard to bring off with full success.

Her suicide is right; and Bresson gets from us, certainly, the 'stock' responses to such a suicide – pity for her, disgust for those who caused it. But, to go back to the point I started on, he quite excludes the often almost inseparable shallower response, the impulse to despair of the world, but rather to luxuriate in hopelessness, as in Shelley's lines 'I could lie down like a tired child / And weep away [this] life of care'. The 'tired child' here does nothing like this. The film gains considerably from the way Mouchette contains in herself so many of the characteristics that in *Diary of a Country Priest* belong to different people. While she shares the priest's isolation, she also has the mysterious, deep, at times even vicious energy of Chantal and Seraphita, and the quiet, gentle worldliness of Dufréty's woman. You can read the earlier film as being critical of the priest and his unworldliness, especially in the final scene at Dufréty's. When he persuades Dufréty to give him absolution, despite being outside the Church, he's not so much redeeming him as strengthening, in death, his own vision of holiness by admitting into it the 'secular' values he has found in this house. And yet, because of the direct way the cinema, as opposed to literature, works, it's hard to respond in this balanced way: the priest's place at the centre of the film is too privileged, and the last shot of the cross too eloquent. It tends to be all or nothing: we attach ourselves uncritically to the priest, or get thoroughly impatient with him, and the film.

The priest's qualities are set against certain others, and an ideal balance can be intellectually inferred; Mouchette contains more of a balance in herself. The priest tries to fight corruption, unsuccessfully; Mouchette doesn't try, but she's only a child, and the sense of other possibilities in the film is strong. Of course the priest does succeed with the Countess, but she dies immediately after, and Bresson's familiar, undramatic way of introducing her death presents it as, once again, a natural consequence. The Countess has been secure in exactly that *order* which the Vicar of Torcy told the priest it was his duty to create. Now, at night, he's reading the letter in which she thanks him for suddenly changing her life; Bresson cuts to his clock showing 6.33 next morning, then tilts down to show his diary note *already written*, with the news of her death. Even if this sequence of shots isn't felt to make a point in itself, the overall implication of the episode is that life is ordered corruption, or chaos, and that purity involves freeing yourself from the world. Despite the Dufrétys, the end of the film sustains this note. *Mouchette* is very different, its end perfectly balanced; I hesitate to labour the comparison between the two films.

In Rossellini's *St Francis* film, the brothers have to decide where they will go to start preaching: they spin round and round to make themselves giddy, and whatever direction they find themselves pointing in when they fall, that way they go. Rossellini's characters submit themselves to the physical way of the world, or to fate, in a child-like acceptance. Mouchette, in rolling down the hill, does something very like this: it is a physical, accepting act, and, though it is suicide, it is life-enhancing in a manner characteristic of Rossellini. In one way it recalls the *St Francis* scene, in another the suicides of the children in *Europe 51* and *Germany Year Zero*. Coming from very different social backgrounds, they, like Mouchette, kill themselves not because they can't cope with living but because others, in the restricted world which they aren't mature enough to be able to leave or change, prevent them from living naturally.

'Through the child the artist could express his awareness of the conflict between human Innocence and the cumulative pressures of social Experience' (Peter Coveney, *The Image of Childhood*). I have long thought that Mr Coveney's admirable study of the way poets and novelists have used children, whether in a positive or a weakly sentimental spirit, could

Still: Mouchette.

profitably be brought up to date, now that the cinema has so largely taken over the central place of the novel, with a chapter on the use of children in films. To set against all the Shirley Temples of the industry, there are four great films at least to make this worth doing: the two Rossellinis, Bergman's *The Silence*, and now *Mouchette*.

UNE FEMME DOUCE

PHIL HARDY

Une femme douce begins with a wife's suicide and ends with the lid of her coffin being screwed into place. The ostensible form of the film is an examination, via the husband's description of the facts that led up to it, of how the suicide came about. An analysis of the film that attempts a simple translation of narrative structure into thematic structure may open well by discussing Bresson's depiction of how communications break down when neither party is able to comprehend the other. But such analysis will inevitably founder on Bresson's persistent refusal throughout the film either to indulge in psychological explanation or to allow his audience to do so. Any examination which proceeds by invocation of the ethos of Bresson's former works leaves us with closed statements about the fate of Man in a fallen world.

The problem with which *Une femme douce* presents us is of examining it in such a way that the end product is neither simply the lowest common denominator of Bresson's films nor a reductivist cliché. There are many starting points from which to proceed: for example, colour – *Une femme douce* is Bresson's first colour film. But the most obvious is to contrast the film with Dostoievsky's novella on which it is based. This has a certain dubious authority in that to some extent it must have been Bresson's starting point. More important, this method has in the past led to useful analyses of Bresson's film (cf. Bazin's essay on *Le journal*

*Still: husband (*Guy Frangin*) and wife (*Dominique Sanda*) in* Une femme douce.

d'un curé de campagne).

Like *Le journal*, *Une femme douce* presents us with a translation into film which is subversively faithful to the original. In his relocation of the novella in time and place, Bresson has faithfully rendered many of the images, the narrative structure and much of the conversation. The changes that have been made are thus doubly significant. In general, whenever Dostoievsky leaves us in no doubt of the 'meaning' of events and offers us indications how to read the symbols, Bresson continually denies us certainty and removes these indications. Thus, in Bresson the girl has no other suitor than the pawnbroker; her choice of marrying him is isolated from social pressures. Similarly, the pawnbroker's past, which is concrete both in meaning and description in Dostoievsky, is shadowed over and made insubstantial in Bresson. At the same time, Bresson, by the bareness of the referential value of the pawnbroker's past seen in terms of *Une femme douce*, refers us back to *Pickpocket* – note the physical resemblance of Guy Frangin to Martin Lassalle. That film, despite its close 'affinities with *Crime and Punishment*' (Daniel Millar, p. 82) provides yet another example of the distance between Bresson's and Dostoievsky's concerns.

Apart from the presence of the wife as a character – in Dostoievsky she is only a corpse – and the introduction of the 'Hamlet' sequence, the two other substantial changes are in the significance of the husband finding his wife with another man, and in Bresson's substitution of the white shawl for the icon. In the film,

127

Dostoievsky's icon is present in the crucifix with the detachable Christ, but its high symbolic value is somewhat reduced: in Dostoievsky the wife leaps to her death clutching the icon; in Bresson, it is her white shawl that floats after her as she falls to her death. In Dostoievsky, the husband hears his wife rejecting her would-be lover; in Bresson we and the husband discover the wife in a compromising situation and then we hear him explaining that his wife was rejecting her companion's advances. His interpretation, correct in Dostoievsky, is thus rendered by Bresson on the same level as his total description of the events leading to his wife's suicide: thoroughly dubious.

One of Dostoievsky's great strength (and indeed a great strength of the nineteenth century novel in general) was that in the absence of any terminology of psychological enquiry, a selective accumulation of detail revealed the psychological nature of the character. In Bresson the details are present (close-ups of objects and limbs, for example) but their psychological undertones are denied them. The wife's comment that the actors in the production of 'Hamlet' have omitted Hamlet's advice to the players to 'o'erstep not the modesty of nature' is pointed. The speech is omitted that the players might, in her words 'bawl their lines'; her husband, in his self-assumed role of Horatio, tells his wife's story melodramatically rather than modestly.

In Bresson, details are not signifiers, as they are in Dostoievsky, but rather containers of meaning, and so constructed that the meaning and its container are inseparable. Just as the street sign that factually reads 'Boulevard Lannes' cannot be wrenched from the Boulevard Lannes and still retain its meaning, so the pawnbroker's interpretation is a false description of the events in the film because it

Still: the couple.

imposes meaning rather than accept the meaning of the events themselves; it is the Boulevard Lannes sign placed in the Champs Elysées.

Accordingly, the things on which Bresson's camera dwells have a substantiality lacked by the characters, especially by that of the husband. Thus, for example, when characters walk up or down stairs, around corners or across rooms, the camera remains on the space they have vacated, not simply to catch their shadows, as often happens, but to record the spaces they pass through. The best illustration of this occurs after the husband has returned to the shop from his visit to the wife's aunts, knowing where his wife has gone. He returns to see if she has returned in his absence. Bresson's camera watches him walk up the first flight of stairs, catches his shadow as it disappears up the second flight and then cuts from the now empty stairs to him in the flat. We see him enter the bathroom and, in close-up, turn off a dripping tap. Then the camera cuts back to include the cake of soap he had once handed to his wife in the bath which now dominates the foreground of the frame. After he has left the bathroom Bresson cuts to show him crossing the living room and, as he leaves the frame, cuts to the bed on which his wife's lingerie is spread out. He enters the frame to sit on the bed, fidgets for a moment and then gets up to leave the flat. At this point, Bresson repeats the sequence of shots that first showed him leaving the apartment and getting into his car to visit the aunts. Consistently throughout this whole sequence Bresson cuts from object to object or from space to space in a solid fashion which contrasts with the wavering path of the pawnbroker that is created by Bresson's precise editing and direction of the actor.

The first step to an understanding of the film is to see at work in the film as a whole the precise editing that regulates the flow of images

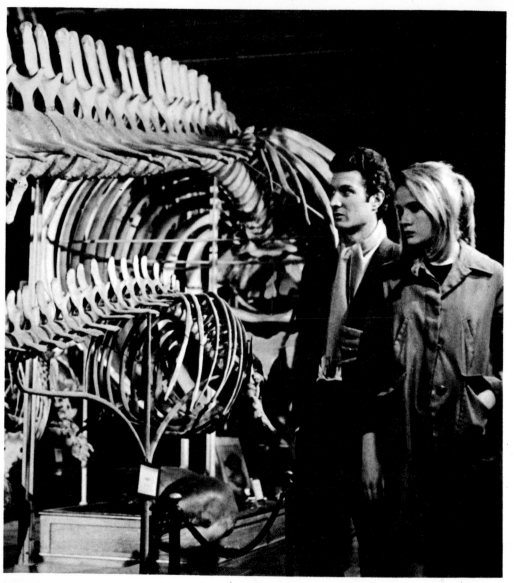

Stills: Une femme douce.

before our eyes. In the double view of the suicide, Bresson suggests the ways we should allow events to make themselves understood. Immediately after the credits, the camera focusses on the outer handle of the glass door into the living room; a hand (Anna's) appears, opens it, and Bresson immediately cuts to inside the room. Through the door on the balcony we see the table crashing down and the chair rocking. The wife has just jumped to her death. The second time we see the events that immediately precede the suicide, we see them from inside the room. After we watch the wife go to the window, the camera cuts to a shot of the inner handle of the door and through the glass we see Anna the housekeeper open the door. Then Bresson places us as he did the first time, in Anna's position, and again we see the table crashing down and the chair rocking. The first time we watch from outside because we are outside the situation. Accordingly Bresson cuts from the crashing table to a shot of the wife's white shawl slowly falling, seen half against the side of the building and half against the blue sky. Over this we hear the naturalistic sound of cars honking and shrieking to a stop. Our first view of the suicide gives us the facts; in our second viewing, having shown us both the suicide and the events that led to it, Bresson directs our attention to its meaning. So, from the crashing table, he cuts to the white shawl falling silently in slow motion against a blue sky.

This shot is inexplicable in itself but seen in the context of the development of the wife's predicament it reveals itself to us in its dual meaning of liberation and death. The image of the white shawl refers us to the shot of the pilot baling out of his 'plane in the Battle of Britain TV documentary watched by the husband when his wife has left the apartment after a quarrel. The image is ironically prefaced by the pawnbroker's remark, 'She was torturing me.' The juxtaposition of the pilot whose parachute offers him his only means of survival with the husband's comment points forward to the sequence in which he attempts to effect a reconciliation with a declaration of forgiveness and love, only to unleash the full anguish of his wife: 'And I thought you were going to leave me.' And so forces her to 'bale out'.

Unlike the *petit-bourgeois* pawnbroker, whose mission in life is to better himself, and whose very job demands a strict application of monetary values to life, the wife is completely unselective; rather she is exhaustive. She plays music unsystematically, following pop with classical music. She likes art of all kinds, from classical nudes to machine art. In a modern art gallery, when her husband refers to a piece of mechanised sculpture as a far cry from painting,

she disagrees, saying that it's all art. She reads voraciously: they meet because she is pawning her possessions to buy books. And, of course, we see her at the cinema and the theatre. Even her strangest interest, in bones, demonstrates her desire for comprehensiveness: she sees bones like those in the skeletons of the prehistoric animals at the museum as being the basic ingredient of all beings.

She wants freedom and privacy, but from the start the pawnbroker intrudes – on her poverty by offering her too much for her icon, on her home by following her there against her wishes, until finally he proposes marriage/captivity to her (their discussion of marriage takes place in front of a cage of monkeys and at one point they are seen from behind the cage, through its wire fence). He offers her 'happiness' and in her reply she acknowledges that she understands the situation. 'You don't want love, you want to marry me.' She succumbs to marriage as in *Balthazar* Marie does to Gérard, and Arnold does to drink. After their discussion there is no intervening period – in the next shot they are being married.

From this point silence becomes the norm. The husband attempts to exercise power over her, to teach her the value of money while she attempts (negatively) to retain her freedom of action and of thought; she continues undeterred in her studies. But the pawnbroker is stronger than she is; she cannot pull the trigger of the gun he holds to his face, but he can, metaphorically, starve her into submission.

And so, slowly, she becomes an object of adoration to her husband as she becomes paler (from her illness) and adds a white shawl (to keep her warm while she convalesces) to her white blouse, until by the end of the film she achieves substantiality in death, so becoming the film's chief object of contemplation – the corpse round which the pawnbroker walks attempting to uncover its meaning.

APPENDIX:INTERVIEW

IAN CAMERON

This interview with Robert Bresson was recorded at the 1962 Cannes Film Festival. Originally intended for broadcasting, the interview was conducted in English. As he wished to avoid any chance of inaccuracies (although he speaks English very well), he insisted on half-an-hour's preparation to jot down any words that he might need and forget during the recording session. We settled down in the lounge of the largest hotel in Cannes to discuss the question over a whisky (mine) and a tonic water (his). Three hours later, many of the questions had been discarded and others completely altered to the questions which Bresson wished to answer. As the whole interview was thus written out before it was recorded, the questions and answers became very terse, and without any of the usual interplay of conversation. Predictably, it was considered unsuitable for broadcasting as it now lacked even the appearance of spontaneity. It sounded not so much like an interview as a Bressonian dialogue.

Why did you wish to add yet another to the number of films made about Joan of Arc?

To make her real and immediate.

What was your principal aim in the film? Was it to show history?

That's the privilege of the cinema – to bring things of the past into the present, providing you avoid the style of the historical films in general. I think the only way to reach the public with historical characters is to show them as if they lived at the present with us. So that was my principal aim.

You never show Joan in the same shot as her accusers. Why?

First, I couldn't do it. The natural decors made it impossible to show them together. But I believe that it is good to create obstacles. For my part I don't work very well without obstacles. Anyway, perhaps even without this difficulty, I would have shown Joan and her accusers in the same way. Because there is only one way of shooting people: from near and in front of them, when you want to know what is happening inside.

Often you seem to place Joan on a light background when her interrogator is on a light background, or to place them both on dark.

That's because it gives a shock to the eye . . . you can't have white in one shot and black in the following one.

The shooting so that each character has his or her shot in the trial sequences gives a feeling not of conflict between Joan and her judges, but of a ritual in which all the participants have their parts to play, parts which they accept.

I don't agree. For me it is a duel between the Bishop Cauchon and Joan. From the beginning to the end, the English and the priests have only the role of witnesses.

You haven't allowed it to become a drama in the normal sense.

My idea is to suggest the things and the feelings also.

What do you expect the audience to bring to your film?

Not their brains but their capacity for feeling.

Do you expect them to know the facts of the trial? Is that why you don't explain who the various participants are?

I never explain anything, as it is done in the theatre.

Or is it that you want the audience to look upon the trial as spectators at a ceremony that is new to them?

This is a good motivation.

Are all your characters in the film those referred to in the historical account of the trial?

They are.

You never show the crowd at the execution except for a couple of shots including their legs. You never show the audience at the trial. Why?

It's a necessity. The sight of a mediaeval crowd would break up the film.

At the beginning of the film we're shown the back of Joan's mother, with a hand on each of her shoulders. Why do you just show her back?

Because I didn't want her to be a character. Besides, it is not in the film itself. It appears before the title.

At the end of the film you stress the tightness of the garment in which she's burnt, that it prevents her from walking properly.

Her garment makes her walk ridiculously, like a little girl. It seems that she's running to the stake.

What's the significance of the gesture when the stone is thrown through the window of her cell? She picks it up and looks at it, at the window and then back at the stone.

She's astonished, but she doesn't care. She's sure till the end that she's to be delivered.

At one point in the trial, the judges make Joan kneel. Then you dissolve away to her standing again afterwards.

The moment of cutting has the same function as that of movement in other films. Shakespeare also cuts at strange times. His cutting is like a door through which the poetry enters.

Why is there so much emphasis placed in the film on Joan being a virgin? Particularly on the attitude of the English to this?

I have shown exactly what I have found in the real account.

There are many shots of doors, open doors. Do these relate to Joan's speech 'If I see a door open,' etc.?

When one is in prison, the most important thing is the door.

The photography is often unusually dark. Is this to establish a sombre mood?

Well, it's important for me to establish the real proportions of light between outside and inside. Outside is very light. Inside more or less dark. The truth about the light takes its part in the general truth of the film.

Why are there a large number of shots of the English peering at Joan through the crack in the cell wall?

There are not as many as you say – as few as possible.

The crack is low down on the wall. You show this by holding the shot on the crack as the observers stand up.

They are sitting down on the other side, which I of course never show. But you may guess that the observers sit down and get up.

When Joan is ill in prison, you show a detail shot first of a priest's hand – the doctor's hand – holding hers when she's ill. Why this detail?

I want to make the public want to see her face before showing it.

Why is it not the Bishop but the two monks in white who inform Joan that she is to die?

One is her confessor. The other is Brother Martin who tried to help her by signs during the trial. The two who have been the closest to her.

There are a number of detailed shots of pens writing the account of the trial. Why have you put these in when she says 'You're writing against me, not for me'?

Because there is a dramatic significance in it. All that is said is written down, and will be taken in general against her. The scratching of

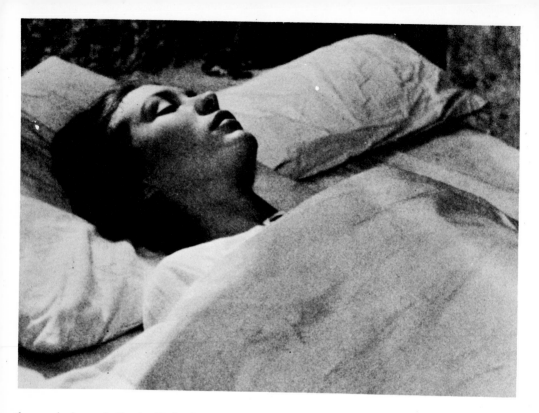

the pen is dramatically significant for me.

Why is the garment she wears at her death brought at the moment when she is receiving the bread at her communion?

The quickness of the end, which is my invention, is for me a dramatic point.

One hardly notices in this film that it is the English soldier who gives Joan the cross. Shaw made quite a lot of this.

This detail is so well known to everybody here in France that I only wanted to suggest it by the sight of his helmet.

Nothing at all is made in the film of the roles of the

English nobleman Warwick and the English priest. Effectively the action involves only Joan and the French priests.

I didn't want to introduce the psychology of Warwick.

Why do you have a shot with a dog in the open as she's about to be burnt?

There's always a dog walking across in the open during a ceremony. The animals feel it when there is something unusual.

Why the details of her clothes being thrown on the fire?

That is very important. They don't want to

leave relics.

You show Joan's feet as she's tripped by one of the crowd. Why do you do this?

That has a certain connection with what happened to Christ when he went to be crucified. I mean the way Christ was mocked and molested.

And the doves which land on the gauze roof of the pavilion?

There is no symbolism in this. I don't like symbolism. It is only to show that life is going on.

Stills: Le procès de Jeanne d'Arc.

Why do you treat the burning partly as a subjective shot of the cross being obscured by smoke?

I think you want me too much to explain what I did.

And, if I could ask you one more question, the reason for the very long held shot at the end just of the stake with chains hanging from it?

Well, it's for me like a miraculous disappearance of Joan.

Your next film I believe will be Lancelot du Lac. *What in particular interests you about Arthurian legends?*

I think it is our mythology as well as yours.

FILMOGRAPHY

Born at Bromont-Lamothe, Puy-de-Dôme, in 1907. Studied classics and philosophy at university, then became a painter. Credited with collaboration on screenplays of *Les Jumeaux de Brighton* (directed by Claude Heymann, 1936) and *Courrier Sud* (directed by Pierre Billon, 1937). Spent a year in a German prisoner-of-war camp.

1934: LES AFFAIRES PUBLIQUES
Directed by Robert Bresson. Produced by Arc Films. Edited by Bresson, Pierre Charbonnier. Music by Jean Wiener.
With: Béby the clown, Marcel Dalio, Gilles Margaritis, Andrée Servilanges.

1943: LES ANGES DU PECHE
Directed by Robert Bresson. Production company: Synops – Roland Tual. Screenplay by Bresson, Father Brückberger; dialogue by Jean Giraudoux. Photographed by Philippe Agostini. Sets by René Renoux. Edited by Yvonne Martin. Music by Jean-Jacques Grünenwald. Assistant director: Frédéric Lictier. Production manager: Dominique Drouin. Paris première: June 23, 1943. 73 minutes.
With: Renée Faure (Anne-Marie), Jany Holt (Thérèse), Sylvie (the Prioress), Mila Parély (Madeleine), Marie-Hélène Dasté (Mother Saint-John), Yolande Laffon (Anne-Marie's mother), Paula Dehelly (Mother Dominique), Sylvia Monfort (Agnès), Gilberte Terbois (Sister Marie-Josèphe), Louis Seigner (prison governor), Georges Colin (prospector), Geneviève Morel (a sister), Christiane Barry (Sister Blaise), Jean Morel (Inspector), Elisabeth Hardy, Andrée Clément, Madeleine Rousset, Claire Olivier, Jacqueline Marbaux (the sisters).

1944: LES DAMES DU BOIS DE BOULOGNE
Directed by Robert Bresson. Production company: Les Films Raoul Ploquin. Screenplay by Bresson, from an episode in Diderot's 'Jacques le Fataliste'; dialogue by Jean Cocteau. Photographed by Philippe Agostini. Sets by Max Douy. Edited by Jean Feyte. Music by Jean-Jacques Grünenwald. Assistant director: Roger Mercanton. Production manager: Robert Lavallée. Paris première: September 21, 1945. 90 minutes.
With: Maria Casarès (Hélène), Elina Labourdette (Agnès), Lucienne Bogaert (her mother), Paul Bernard (Jean), Jean Marchat (Jacques), Bernard Lajarrige, Marcel Rouze, Emma Lyonel, Lucy Lancy, Mme de Morlay.

1950: LE JOURNAL D'UN CURE DE CAMPAGNE – *Diary of a Country Priest*.
Directed by Robert Bresson. Production company: U.G.C. Screenplay by Bresson from the novel by Georges Bernanos; dialogue by Bresson. Photographed by Léonce-Henry Burel. Sets by Pierre Charbonnier. Edited by Paulette Robert. Music by Jean-Jacques Grünenwald. Assistant director: Guy Lefranc. Production manager: Robert Sussfield. 120 minutes.

Still: Martin Lassalle in Pickpocket.

With: Claude Laydu (priest), Nicole Maurey (Louise), Nicole Ladmiral (Chantal), Marie-Monique Arkell, alias Rachel Bérendt (Countess), Jean Riveyre (the Count), Serge Bento (Mitonnet), Jean Danet (Olivier), Martine Lemaire (Séraphita), Guibert (priest at Torcy), Léon Arvel (Fabregard), Yvette Etiévant (housekeeper), Gaston Séverin (Canon), Bernard Hubrenne (Dufrěty), Germaine Stainval (café owner), Gilberte Terbois (Mlle Dumouchal), Morange, François Valorbe, Antoine Balpêtre (doctor).

1956: UN CONDAMNE A MORT S'EST ECHAPPE or LE VENT SOUFFLE OU IL VEUT – *A Man Escaped.*
Directed by Robert Bresson. Produced by Sociéte Nouvelle des Etablissements Gaumont-Nouvelles Editions de Films (Alain Poiré, Jean Thuillier). Screenplay adapted by Bresson, from the account by André Devigny; dialogue by Bresson. Photographed by Léonce-Henry Burel. Sets by Pierre Charbonnier. Edited by Raymond Lamy. Music from Mozart, Mass in C minor. Assistant director: Michel Clément. Production manager: Robert Sussfield. 102 minutes.
With: François Leterrier (Lt Fontaine), Charles LeClainche (Jost), Maurice Beerblock (Blanchet), Roland Monod (Revd de Leiris), Jacques Ertaud (Orsini), Jean-Paul Delhumeau (Hebrard), Roger Tréherne (Terry), Jean-Philippe Delamare (Prisoner 110), Jacques Oerlemans (Chief Warder), Klaus Detlef Grevenhorst (German Intelligence officer), Leonhard Schmidt (German escort).

1959: PICKPOCKET
Directed by Robert Bresson. Produced by Agnès Delahaie. Screenplay by Bresson. Photographed by Léonce-Henry Burel. Sets by Pierre Charbonnier. Edited by Raymond Lamy. Music by Jean-Baptiste Lully. Production manager:

Annie Dorfmann. 75 minutes.
With: Martin Lassalle (Michel), Pierre Leymarie (Jacques), Jean Pelegri (Police Inspector), Marika Green (Jeanne), Kassagi (1st accomplice), Pierre Etaix (2nd accomplice), Dolly Scal (Michel's mother), Pelegri, Sophie Saint-Just.

1961: LE PROCES DE JEANNE D'ARC – *The Trial of Joan of Arc.*
Directed by Robert Bresson. Produced by Agnès Delahaie. Screenplay by Bresson from the minutes of the trial and rehabilitation. Photographed by Léonce-Henry Burel. Sets by Pierre Charbonnier, costumes by Lucilla Mussini. Edited by Germaine Artus. Music by Francis Seyrig. Assistant Director: Serge Roullet. Production manager: Leon Sanz. 65 minutes.
With: Florence Delay, alias Carrez (Joan), Jean-Claude Fourneau (Cauchon), Marc Jacquier (Jane Lemaître), Roger Honorat (Jean Beaupère), Jean Gillibert (Jean de Chatillon), André Régnier (d'Estivet), Michel Herubel (Brother Isambart de la Pierre), Jean Darbaud (Nicolas de Houppeville), Richard Pratt (Warwick), Michael Williams (Englishman), Harry Sommers (Bishop of Winchester), Donald O'Brien (English priest), Gérard Zingg (Jean Lohier), Andre Maurice (Tiphaine), Robert Nimet (Guillaume Erard), Yves Leprince (Pierre Morice), Arthur le Bau (Jean Massieu), Philippe Dreux (Brother Martin Ladvenu).

1966: AU HASARD, BALTHAZAR – *Balthazar*
Directed by Robert Bresson. Production company: Argos Films, Parc Film, Athos Films (Paris), Svensk-Filmindustri, Svensk Filminstitutet. Produced by Mag Bodard. Screenplay by Bresson. Photographed by Ghislain Cloquet. Sets by Pierre Charbonnier. Edited by Raymond Lamy. Music: Franz Schubert, Piano

Sonata No. 20; Jean Wiener. Assistant directors: Jacques Kebadian, Sven Frostenson. Production manager: Philippe Dussart. 95 minutes.

With: Anne Wiazemsky (Marie), François Lafarge (Gérard), Philippe Asselin (school master), Nathalie Joyaut (Marie's mother), Walter Green (Jacques), J.-C. Guilbert (Arnold) François Sullerot (baker), M. C. Frémont (baker's wife), Pierre Klossowski (corn merchant), Jean Remignard (notary), Jacques Sorbets (Captain of police), Tord Paag (Louis), Sven Frostenson, Roger Fjellstrom (naughty boys), Jean-Joel Barbier (dean), Remy Brozeck (Marcel), Mylène Weyergans (nurse), Guy Brejac (veterinary surgeon).

1966: MOUCHETTE

Directed by Robert Bresson. Produced by Parc Film/Argos Films (Anatole Dauman). Screenplay by Bresson from 'Nouvelle Histoire de Mouchette' by Georges Bernanos. Photographed by Ghislain Cloquet. Sets by Pierre Guffroy. Edited by Raymond Lamy. Music: Monteverdi, 'Magnificat'; song by Jean Wiener. Assistant directors: Jacques Kebadian, Mylène van der Mersch. Production managers: Philippe Dussart, Michel Choquet. 90 minutes.

With: Nadine Nortier (Mouchette) Jean-Claude Guilbert (Arsène), Maria Cardinal (mother), Paul Hébert (father), Jean Vimenet (Gamekeeper, Mathieu), Marie Suzini (Mathieu's wife), Raymond Chabrun (grocer), Suzanne Huguenin (layer out of the dead), Marie Trichet (Louisa).

1969: UNE FEMME DOUCE – *A Gentle Creature*

Directed by Robert Bresson. Produced by Parc Film/Marianne Productions (Mag Bodard). Screenplay by Bresson from a story by Dostoievsky. Photographed in Eastmancolor by Ghislain Cloquet. Sets by Pierre Charbonnier.

Edited by Raymond Lamy. Assistant director: Jacques Kebadian. 87 minutes. First shown Paris, June 17, 1969.

With: Dominique Sanda (girl), Guy Frangin (man), Jane Lobre (Anna).

BIBLIOGRAPHY

BOOKS AND PAMPHLETS DEVOTED TO BRESSON

BRIOT, René: *Robert Bresson*. Paris, Editions du Cerf, 1957.

CANZIANI, Alfonso: *Un maestro del cinema francese: Robert Bresson*. Milan, Silva Editore, 1965.

COLLET, Jean: *Le drôle de chemin de Bresson à Balthazar*. Paris, Etudes, 1966. (Pamphlet reprinted from *Etudes Cinématographiques*.)

DROGUET, Robert: *Robert Bresson*. Lyon, Premier Plan 42, SERDOC, 1966.

ESTEVE, Michel: *Robert Bresson*. Paris, Seghers, 1962. (*Cinéma D'Aujourd'hui* no. 8.)

SEMOLUE, Jean: *Bresson*. Paris, Editions Universitaires, 1959. (*Classiques du Cinéma* no. 7.)

BOOKS WITH SECTIONS ON BRESSON

ARMES, Roy: 'Robert Bresson.' [In *French cinema since 1946*. Vol. 1. London, Zwemmer; New York, A. S. Barnes, 1966.]

LEPROHON, Pierre: 'Robert Bresson.' [In *Présences contemporaines: cinéma*. Paris, Nouvelles Editions Debresse, 1957.]

MAURIAC, Claude: 'Robert Bresson.' [In *Petite littérature du cinéma*. Paris, Editions du Cerf, 1957.]

RHODE, Eric: 'Robert Bresson.' [In *Tower of Babel*. Weidenfeld & Nicolson, 1966.]

SARRIS, Andrew (editor): *Interviews with Film Directors*, 1967 (interview reprinted from *Movie 7*).

TAYLOR, John Russell: 'Robert Bresson.' [In *Cinema eye, cinema ear: some key filmmakers of the sixties*. Methuen, 1964.]

BOOK MATERIAL ON INDIVIDUAL FILMS

Les Dames du Bois de Boulogne

CHEVALLIER, Jacques: 'Les Dames du Bois de Boulogne.' [In *Regards neufs sur le cinéma*. Edited by Jacques Chevallier and Max Egly. Paris, Editions du Seuil, 1963.]

FONG, Monique: 'Les Dames du Bois de Boulogne.' [In *Analyse de films*. Paris, IDHEC, 1948.]

GUTH, Paul: *Autour des Dames du Bois de Boulogne*. Paris, René Juillard, 1945.

Le Journal d'un Curé de Campagne

ESTEVE, Michel: 'Mazarin et le journal d'un curé de campagne: la Passion du Christ refusée et acceptée.' [In *La Passion du Christ comme thème cinématographique*. Edited by Michel Estève. Paris, Lettres Modernes, 1961.]

LUDMAN, René: 'Grâce et déréliction: journal d'un curé de campagne.' [In *Cinéma: foi et morale*. Paris, Editions du Cerf, 1956.]

McANANY, Emile G., and WILLIAMS, Robert: 'Diary of a country priest.' [In *The filmviewer's handbook*. Glen Rock (New Jersey), Paulist Press, 1965.]

Un Condamné a mort c'est échappé

JACOB, Gilles: 'Le condamné a mort c'est échappé, ou, le vent souffle ou il veut.' [In *Le cinéma moderne*. Lyon, SERDOC, 1964.]

Pickpocket

ESTEVE, Michel: 'Pickpocket: permanence de Robert Bresson.' [In *Etudes Cinématographiques* nos. 3-4; edited by Henri Agel and Georges-Albert Astre. Paris, Lettres Modernes, 1960.]

Proces de Jeanne d'Arc

ESTEVE, Michel (editor): 'Jeanne d'Arc à l'écran.' [In *Etudes Cinématographiques* nos. 18-19. Paris, Lettres Modernes, 1962.] Includes a long interview with Bresson about the film.

PERIODICAL ARTICLES ON BRESSON

Cahiers du cinéma no. 50, Aug.-Sept. 1955.
Julien Green: 'En travaillant avec Robert Bresson' (on the script for '*Ignace de Loyola*').

Cahiers du cinéma no. 75, Oct. 1957.
'Propos de Robert Bresson: sténographie d'une conférence de presse.'
Jean Sémolué: 'Les personages de Robert Bresson'.

Cahiers du cinéma no. 104, Feb. 1960.
Jacques Doniol-Valcroze and Jean-Luc Godard: 'Entretien avec Robert Bresson' (with particular reference to '*Pickpocket*').

Cahiers du cinéma no. 140. Feb. 1963.
Yves Kovacs: 'Entretien avec Robert Bresson' (with particular reference to '*Procès de Jeanne d'Arc*').

Cahiers du cinéma no. 178, May 1966.
Jean-Luc Godard and Michel Delahaye: 'La question: entretien avec Robert Bresson'; translated in *Cahiers* in English, no. 8.

Cahiers du cinéma no. 211, April 1969.
Jean-Pierre Oudart: 'La Suture'.

Cineforum, Sept. 1967.
Jean Sémolué: 'Mouchette – L'Evoluzione di Uno Stile'.
Michel Estève: 'Da Bernanos a Bresson.'

Cinema '63 no. 73, Feb. 1963.
'Le dossier du mois: Robert Bresson.'
Filmographie.

Ecran Francais, Oct. 1945.
Jacques Becker: 'Hommage à Robert Bresson'.

Filmcritica nos. 147-8, 1964.
Eduardo Bruno: 'Ordine Razionale in Robert Bresson'.

Film Culture no. 20, 1959.
Richard Roud: 'The early work of Robert Bresson'.

Film Quarterly, vol. XIII, no. 3, Spring 1960.
Marjorie Green: 'Robert Bresson'.

Image et Son, no. 156, Nov. 1962.
Philippe Durand: 'Le Drôle de Chemin de Robert Bresson'. Dossiers of quotations on Bresson and his films.
Jacques Chevallier (editor): 'Fiche on *Les Dames du Bois de Boulogne*'.

Image et Son no. 210, March 1967.
Jean Vimenet: 'Apparence de R. Bresson: entretien'.

Positif nos. 3, 4, 5 (1952-3).
Bernard Chardère: 'A Propos de Bresson: Un Art de Suggestion des Visage à L'Ame'.

Seventh Art, Summer, 1964.
Susan Sontag: 'Spiritual Style in the Films of Robert Bresson'. (Reprinted in *Against Interpretation; and other essays*. New York, Farrar, Straus & Giroux, 1966.)

Sight and Sound, vol. 23, no. 1, July-Sept. 1953.
Gavin Lambert: 'Notes on Robert Bresson'.

Sight and Sound, vol. 27, no. 1, Summer 1957.
Roland Monod: 'Working with Bresson' (translation of article published in *Cahiers du Cinéma* no. 64, Nov. 1956).

Télé-Ciné no. 25, 1950.
'L'Oeuvre de Robert Bresson' – issue devoted to Bresson.

SCRIPTS

Les Dames du Bois de Boulogne
Cahiers du Cinéma no. 75, Oct. 1957; no. 76, Nov. 1957; no. 77, Dec. 1957.
Jean Cocteau: 'Les Dames du Bois de Boulogne: dialogue'.

Procès de Jeanne d'Arc
BRESSON, Robert: *Procès de Jeanne d'Arc: film*. Paris, René Juillard, 1962.

Au hasard, Balthazar
Cineforum no. 56, 1966. Sceneggiatura originale e integrale del film 'Au hasard, Balthazar'.

Mouchette
L'Avant Scène du Cinéma, April 1968. (In Italian in *Cineforum*, Sept. 1967.)

Still on p. 144: Elina Labourdette and Paul Bernard in Les Dames du Bois de Boulogne.